W9-CNJ-473

VERIFICATION METHODOLOGY MANUAL

Techniques for Verifying HDL Designs

David Dempster   **Michael Stuart**

Published by Teamwork International

Cover design: Joanna Watkinson of Blue Pepper Designs

Cover-montage photographs used with permission of copyright owner.

Interior design: Teamwork International.

Illustrations: Chris Moses of TransEDA.

Teamwork International,
New Century House,
Stable View, Yateley,
Hampshire, GU46 7SF
United Kingdom
Int. Tel: +44 1252-665-924
Int. Fax: +44 1252-692-706
E-mail: info@teamwork-int.com
Web site: www.teamwork-int.com

Contents

Chapter 1. Overview of Front-End Tools

Chapter 2. Code and Rule Checking in the Design Flow

Chapter 3. Introduction to Coverage Analysis

Chapter 11. Overview of Test Bench Requirements

Chapter 12. Analyzing and Optimizing the Test Suite

Appendix A. On-line Resources and Further Reading

Appendix F. Dynamic Property Checking - Worked Examples

Appendix G. Creating Properties - Worked Examples

Glossary

Index

FOREWORD

A year ago I wrote about the emerging "verification crisis" caused by the dramatically increasing difficulty of functional verification of complex ICs. This crisis is no longer emerging; we are living with it today and it continues to grow in severity. In fact, the 2001 International Technology Roadmap for Semiconductors states, "Without major breakthroughs, verification will be a non-scalable, show-stopping barrier to further progress in the semiconductor industry." Fortunately, creative new approaches to verification are emerging that promise to break through the barrier and to allow the show to go on.

One of the most promising trends is that of property checking and the use of properties as a standard representation of design intent. As this third edition of the Verification Methodology Manual goes to print, Accellera is voting on an industry-standard property language. With the establishment of this open standard, IP vendors, SOC developers and EDA companies will for the first time have a common language for describing desired design behavior independently from design implementation. This language will enable a new generation of formal, semi-formal and dynamic verification tools to emerge that leverage a unified description of design intent and dramatically raise verification productivity. It will also enable the emergence of a "property economy", where property libraries become another component of verification IP that promote verification reuse and speed the verification of cores when integrated in systems.

This edition of the Verification Methodology Manual includes a section on dynamic property checking, a new technique that enables properties to be verified in simulation at any level of design integration. Dynamic property checking complements code coverage in helping determine the completeness of a design's verification. It also complements formal property checking by providing a measurable degree of confidence for properties that cannot be checked formally. This book does contain some references to TransEDA products, but is meant as a general reference to design and verification engineers everywhere. I hope you find it informative and useful.

Ellis Smith
Chief Executive Officer, TransEDA
Los Gatos, California April 15, 2002

ABOUT THE AUTHORS

David Dempster has worked in the CAE and EDA industry for over 18-years in an applications engineering and training role. He worked for a number of years with Valid Logic Systems and Cadence Design Systems developing and presenting end-user technical training programmes before starting his own design consultancy and management training company. David's work as a management-training consultant has taken him to the four corners of the globe supporting most of the leading-edge electronic and computing companies. David has travelled extensively in the USA, Japan, Korea, Taiwan, Europe and Scandinavia presenting technical workshops on coverage analysis methodology and design tools. During the last two years he has worked very closely with TransEDA developing their customer education training programmes and supporting their exhibitions and road-shows.

Michael Stuart is the Director of Customer and Technical Support at TransEDA. He is a founder member of TransEDA and has held a number of Product Marketing and Customer Support positions at TransEDA including Product Manager for the VeriSure coverage analysis tool. Before joining TransEDA Michael worked as a development Engineer for Veda Design Automation and Siemens (formerly Plessey). Michael holds a first class honours degree in Electronic and Electrical Engineering from Robert Gordon's Institute of Technology, Aberdeen.

ACKNOWLEDGEMENTS

It is very tempting to feel that you have to thank everyone that you have ever met in your whole life when compiling the mandatory acknowledgements page. So apart from our chauffeurs, personal hairstylists and house designers, may we single out the following people and pieces of technology for a special mention.

First of all may we convey our thanks to the sales and marketing team at TransEDA who had the original concept for the creation of the Verification Methodology Manual and for keeping us focused and on-track during the compilation phase of the manuscript.

We are also indebted to the senior managers, programmers and technical support personnel at TransEDA for allowing us free use of their coverage analysis tools and workstations, and for giving us unlimited access to their technology, in-depth documentation and research papers. May we also thank Chris Rose at Saros Technology for providing us with a copy of ModelSim 5.5 from Model Technology (now owned by Mentor Graphics) that enabled us to simulate all the worked examples that are referenced in this manual.

We would also like to thank Thomas Borgstrom (Vice President, Marketing at TransEDA) and Jeffrey Barkley (Marketing Manager at TransEDA) for their valuable contribution to the two chapters entitled - *FSM Coverage* and *Dynamic Property Checking*.

Thanks must also go to Chris Moses, of TransEDA, for his graphical expertise and hard work turning our rough sketches into drawings that illustrated so clearly the information we wanted to convey.

We would also like to acknowledge the contribution that the Internet made to our work by enabling us both to stay in communication with each other and to provide the review team with regular 'copy' while we held down full-time jobs which involved a considerable amount of travel visiting customers worldwide.

Michael would like to thank his wife, Sheila for her support, encouragement and typing skills.

Finally we would like to thank Adobe Inc. for producing FrameMaker, the excellent desktop publishing and document management package that enabled us to seamlessly create a book out of a series of individual chapters, authors' rough notes and random thoughts.

David Dempster and Michael Stuart

PREFACE

This manual has been specifically designed to help and support:

- Experienced circuit designers who use the Verilog or VHDL hardware description languages, and are interested in increasing the productivity and quality of their work.

- Engineering managers or project leaders who are seriously considering the benefits and implications of incorporating coverage analysis tools in the design flow.

- Verification and test engineers who are responsible for proving that a design completely meets its specification prior to sign-off.

- Engineers involved in evaluating EDA design tools who require an in-depth understanding of how these tools operate and the benefits that can be achieved.

Although Chapter 3 covers a brief introduction to coverage analysis concepts, as applied to software programming languages, it is assumed that the reader will be familiar with the basic operation of the Verilog or VHDL hardware design languages.

If you are unfamiliar with coverage analysis tools then you should read carefully through each chapter and try out the worked examples in Appendices B to G. This approach should enable you to build up a good understanding of the concepts of coverage analysis as applied to the Verilog and VHDL hardware description languages. It will also provide you with an opportunity to acquire some first-hand practical experience in the use of these tools.

Experienced designers and verification engineers will probably find Chapters 6 thru 12 a useful starting point. These chapters cover the practicalities of applying coverage analysis measurements to HDL source code; how to interpret the results obtained with these tools, and how to manage/optimize the test suite.

If you are an engineering manager or project leader you could start by reading Chapters 4, 5 and 7. This will enable you to find out how coverage analysis tools can be used in the design flow and appreciate some of the benefits that can be achieved with these tools. Chapters 6, 9, 10 and 12 should then be studied in order to understand the practicalities of applying a coverage analysis tool to a project.

If you are planning to carry out an evaluation of a coverage analysis tool you will find that Appendices A to G contains some useful reference material and access to a number of on-line resources.

Chapter 1

Overview of Front-End Tools

CIRCUIT DESIGN CAN BE A RISKY BUSINESS

In a number of companies the procedures that are used to design complex integrated circuits can be summarised as giving the people that have to use them a mixture of excitement and frustration. Designers get excited when things go well and results match or exceed their expectation levels. Equally, it is frustrating when things go wrong and additional time is required making changes to a design to meet the specification. So what can be done to ensure that every design is... *right first time?*

At the simplistic level there are probably at least two answers to this question. The first is to establish a set of procedures that encourage designers to apply quality standards to each stage of the design process. The second is to complement those procedures with tools that reinforce the quality standards by verifying that the design is correct at each stage of development. On paper this may sound fairly obvious and straightforward but in reality there are a number of factors that can occur to disrupt this strategy. For example, project time scales are normally very tight because a company needs to ensure its product reaches the market place before its competitor otherwise market share will be lost. This means there is probably very little time allocated for making other than minor corrections to the design. Major changes or last minute improvements to the design-specification can cause a dilemma for the project manager as a decision has to be made as to whether to incorporate the changes, and maybe miss the release date, or risk launching an inferior product.

THE FRONT TO BACK DESIGN ROUTE

The usual sequence a designer goes through when developing an integrated circuit is shown pictorially in Figure 1-1.

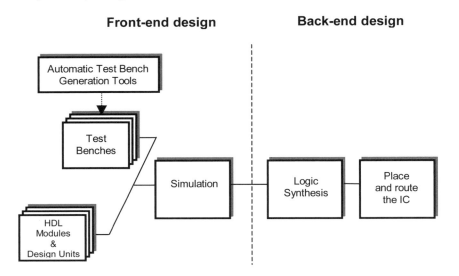

Figure 1-1

In broad terms the steps can be classified as:

Stage 1.
Capturing a description of the design using a HDL (Hardware Description Language). (e.g. Verilog or VHDL.)

Note: If the reader requires any background information about hardware description languages then *Appendix A - On-Line Resources and Further Reading* should be consulted.

Stage 2.
Simulating the design to prove that it works correctly and meets specification.

Stage 3.
Logic synthesis, where the design-description is converted into a physical gate description.

Stage 4.
Organising the layout of the integrated circuit to satisfy various physical and electrical constraints. (e.g. power dissipation, pin-to-pin delays, electrical loading, etc.)

The remainder of this chapter will examine the problems that can occur during stages 1 and 2 and identify some tools that can help overcome these potential problems.

Starting at the front-end, the first step that needs to be performed is the design-capture of each module or design unit and development of the relevant test benches. Tools to achieve these tasks range from simple text editors through to sophisticated code/rule checkers. Graphical entry methods can also be used - especially if a design contains one or more complex finite state machines. The objective at this stage is to ensure that the syntax and semantics of the HDL code written by the designer are correct. Any coding errors not picked up at this stage will be passed through to the simulation process which could have serious consequences as undetected coding errors may cause the simulation to fail or produce spurious results. In either case the result is wasted simulation time and frustration for the designer.

Further details regarding various design capture methods and their benefits can be found in *Chapter 2 - Code and Rule Checking in the Design Flow.*

Once the HDL code is correct a designer can safely move onto the second stage and start the simulation process. Modules that represent self-contained parts of the design can be simulated as soon as they have been captured. Other modules, that rely on receiving signals from other parts of the design, may require a dedicated test bench to be created in order to be simulated. Alternatively the simulation of these modules could be postponed until all the other relevant and dependent modules have been captured. This approach should be avoided wherever possible because potentially untested modules are being incorporated into the design at the sub-system testing phase. The overall effect of using this particular technique will be to increase the amount of testing that needs to be done at the sub-system integration level.

It can be tempting for a designer to move on to stage 3 and start the synthesis process as soon as all the parts of the design have been successfully simulated. This is an understandable reaction because a number of designers believe that if a design simulates correctly then that means it will work correctly. This assumption is correct provided a designer has rigorously checked that all parts of the design have been fully exercised with a comprehensive or exhaustive set of test data. At the fundamental level this means establishing that all executable statements in the design have been executed and that all the decision-branches have been taken. Normally it is quite difficult for a designer to manually estimate what percentage of the design has been covered. One solution to the problem is to make use of a coverage analysis tool at this stage to help determine which parts of the design have not been covered or fully exercised. The results obtained from coverage analysis tools can be used to improve productivity and enhance quality by directing a designer to parts of the design where the coverage is poor or inadequate.

Various chapters in this manual are devoted to giving an in-depth explanation of the fundamentals of coverage analysis, the practical value of coverage analysis and the different types of measurements that can be applied to a design.

Figure 1-2 shows how HDL checking and coverage analysis can be incorporated into the first two stages of the design flow.

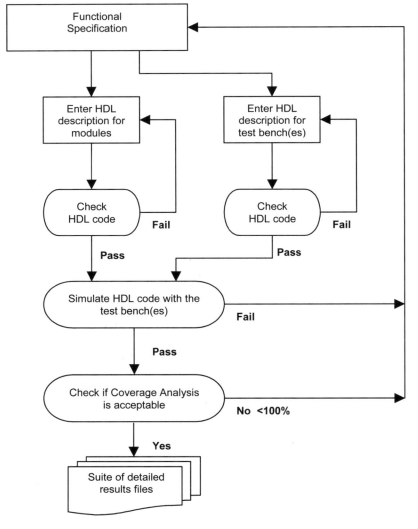

Figure 1-2

HANDLING DESIGN CHANGES

One of the most time-consuming tasks a designer has to do involves making changes
to a design and then checking that those changes do not adversely affect other parts of
the design. Consider the situation, shown by Figure 1-3, where a suite of test benches
is used to exercise different parts of a design which comprises of a set of HDL files.
In reality the number of test benches that are used may run into hundreds or even
thousands and may involve a considerable amount of simulation time if all the test
benches were to be re-run whenever a design-change occurred.

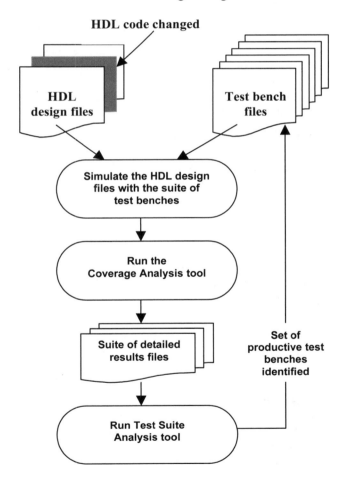

Figure 1-3

Another factor that needs to be taken into consideration is the fact that, usually, there is a certain amount of overlap between one test bench and another. For example, although a designer will normally try to write a test bench to check a certain part of the design, it is quite possible that one test maps over parts of the design that have already been checked. This means that the majority of test benches are not normally unique unless a lot of time is devoted to planning and implementing an efficient testing strategy.

At the end of the simulation phase the information that is contained in the suite of detailed results files shows the amount of coverage that has been achieved by each test bench. Taking all the above factors into consideration it should therefore be possible to drastically reduce the amount of simulation time by selecting the test benches that are the most productive and running just those test benches.

An extremely powerful tool that can used to calculate which test benches are the most productive is the test suite optimizer. This particular tool takes the information, produced by the coverage analysis tool, and ranks that information according to which test bench produced the highest amount of coverage in the shortest simulation time. Armed with this information a designer can optimize the test suite by:

- Running the most productive test benches first, and

- Removing the non-productive test benches or the ones that map over parts of the design that have already been tested.

SUMMARY

In summary, this chapter has introduced the following tools that can be used to enhance the quality and productivity of the front-end design process.

- HDL code checking

- Coverage analysis

- Test suite analysis

This chapter has also explained that catching and isolating coding and coverage problems early in the design cycle can dramatically reduce a project's overall development time. Also the technique whereby the results from a set of test benches are analyzed and used to identify which are the most productive ones, has been introduced as an effective method of saving valuable simulation time. Each of these topics is described in greater detail and related to actual worked examples in the various chapters that follow.

Chapter 2

Code and Rule Checking in the Design Flow

HDL CAPTURE TOOLS

As stated in Chapter 1, one of the first tasks a designer needs to do is capture a description of the design using a HDL (Hardware Description Language). e.g. Verilog or VHDL. The objective at this stage is to create high-quality code as quickly as possible before moving on to the simulation stage. As design capture can be a very time consuming and error prone process, there are a number of tools that can help a designer improve productivity and enhance the quality of the HDL code produced at this stage.

These tools can be classified as:

- Text editors

- Linters

- Graphical editors

- Rule-based checkers

TEXT EDITORS

Nearly everyone, at one time or another, has used a text editor to create or alter a piece of ASCII text and discovered that the basic text editors offer simple facilities such as the ability to copy and paste text, search and replace text strings and format text using tabs (tabulation characters) or spaces.

Some of the more advanced text editors enable text to be automatically indented and color-coded whenever certain keywords or constructs are detected. Although this facility is useful, because it shows the structure of the captured code, it does not help in isolating and identifying any coding problems or syntax errors. (e.g. a missing semicolon (;) symbol at the end of a line or an opening or closing quote (') mark omitted from a text string.)

There are also programmable editors that have language specific modes of operation that automate and enforce a standard set of coding standards. This is normally achieved by using a predefined template that specifies the coding standards that will be used by the editor. As the information held in the template is fixed it is not very easy for the user to make changes to the defined coding standards.

LINTERS

The original concept of 'linting' comes from languages like C and C++ where linters are used to check for inconsistencies within the code that had been written. For example, checking that a value passed to a procedure or function was the correct type (i.e. integer, boolean, string, etc.) and that it matched what had been declared in the main body of the program. Linters were also used to check for possible portability problems when code was moved from one implementation of C to another. (e.g. K & R to ANSI C.) Because Verilog and VHDL have a syntax very similar to C and Pascal respectively, it was natural for linters to appear for these two HDL languages.

VHDL is a strongly typed language and this means it is relatively easy task for a linting tool to check for any inconsistencies in the source code. Verilog on the other hand is a loosely typed language that allows registers to be overloaded or array boundaries to be exceeded. So here the linting tool has to detect "logical" coding errors that would otherwise be acceptable to Verilog. A simple example of this type of coding error is shown below where a vectored net is assigned to a signal of a different width.

```
a[0]  <=  #1  b[1:0]
```

Depending upon the sophistication of the linting tool, other forms of checks that may be applied include: range and index checking, checking whether a variable is used before it has been assigned and width checking.

GRAPHICAL EDITORS

Consider the task of capturing a complex FSM (Finite State Machine) containing a large number of states and conditional transitions. In this situation a designer is normally faced with the task of writing a series of involved 'case' constructs where each 'case term' defines a state and the conditions that must be satisfied in order to move onto the next state. Although a designer may be willing to undertake this task at the initial design stage, it can get very tedious and time-consuming altering the HDL code whenever changes are made to the operational sequence of the FSM. In this particular situation graphical editors can prove very useful, because as well as saving time at the design capture stage they also present the designer with a pictorial image of the FSM that makes it easier to understand the interactions within the FSM.

For example, consider the state diagram shown in Figure 2-1. It is normally easier to see the interactions between the various states using a graphical presentation than trying to decipher a block of HDL source code that may span a number of printed pages.

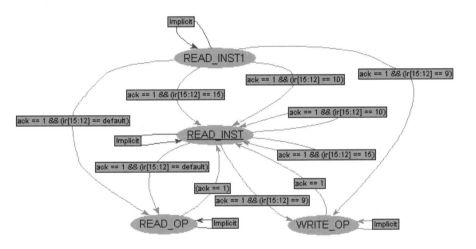

Figure 2-1

RULE-BASED CHECKERS

Rule-based checkers, unlike the simple linting tools with fixed rules, make extensive use of configurable rules to check the quality of the HDL code produced at the design capture stage. As the number of rules that are available with these types of checkers can be extensive, it is normal practice to organise the rules into rule-sets or lists that relate to certain aspects of a designer's work. For example, a selection of the rules could be gathered together to specify how HDL constructs should be coded. Another rule-set might contain rules that refer to things such as allowable file name suffixes, number of modules per file and the maximum line-length of the HDL source code. Other rule-sets may be needed in a company to ensure that corporate standards such as documentation procedures and naming conventions are correctly applied by all the design engineers.

Some examples of the typical content for the above rule-sets are given below.

- Coding rules
    * Each VHDL architecture should have only one clock.
    * Clocked designs must be synchronised on the rising edge of a clock signal.
    * In a finite state machine, for each state there must be a defined next state with an associated output value.
    * 'Case' statements must be complete (i.e. contain a default or a when others clause).

- Style rules
    * The length of a text line should not exceed 100 characters.
    * Each line should only contain a single VHDL/Verilog statement.

- Documentation rules
    * Each HDL source file must contain a comment block.
    * The start of each control block (e.g. always block) must be commented.

- Naming rules
    * Each clock signal must start with the prefix 'clk'.
    * All active high signals must end with the suffix '_h'.

The concept of having dedicated rule-sets can be taken a stage further by combining a selection of the individual rules from one or more of the rule-sets to form a rule-database or rule-category. For example, the following rule-databases could be constructed for a specific HDL (e.g. Verilog or VHDL) by carefully choosing specific rules from the established rule-sets.

- Best Practices
  As the name implies this rule-database contains rules that represent good HDL coding practices as applied to Verilog or VHDL.

- RMM
  This rule-database contains rules that reflect the guidelines that appear in the book entitled *Reuse Methodology Manual*. (See *Appendix-A On-Line Resources and Further Reading* for more details regarding this publication.)

- OpenMORE
  The rules in this rule-database are effectively the same as the set of rules in the RMM rule-database. The main difference is that a score is applied to each rule in accordance with the OpenMORE design scoring system devised by Synopsys and Mentor Graphics. Points are awarded whenever a rule is successfully achieved. No points are awarded if a rule is broken. At the end of the checking process the overall number of points that have been scored indicates the quality factor or 'goodness' of the design.

- Synthesis
  The rules in this rule-database perform checks to ensure that the HDL code that has been used in the design is synthesizable. This particular rule-database is very useful as it can avoid wasting time at the synthesis stage trying to synthesize non-compliant code.

- Portability
  This rule-database contains rules to check that HDL code is transportable from Verilog to VHDL or from VHDL to Verilog. This particular rule-database is very useful in situations where dual languages are used within the same company.

Although the above set of rule-databases should cater for the majority of tasks a designer will encounter, there may be occasions where a specialised rule-database is required to satisfy a specific design-constraint or project requirement. This can be accomplished by constructing a custom rule-database by selecting one or more rules from any of the existing rule-databases and then, if needed, adding additional dedicated rules (that have been previously written) to extend the overall effectiveness of the rule-database.

An example of a specialised rule database may be one that contains rules that represent a proprietary DFT (Design For Test) methodology.

Figure 2-2 shows how basic rules are grouped into rules-sets (e.g. Coding rules, Style rules, Documentation rules, Naming rules) and how the rule-sets can be combined together to form rule-databases.

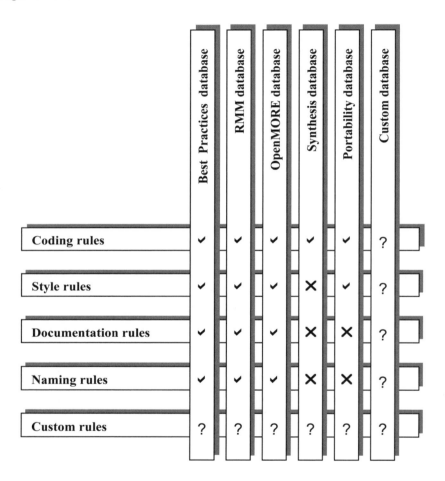

Figure 2-2

At the start of this section it was mentioned that rule-based checkers make extensive use of configurable rules. Because there are various ways in which each basic rule could be configured some examples of how this can be achieved are listed on the following pages.

RULE CHECKING AND THE DESIGN HIERARCHY

In addition to configurability the other fundamental difference which distinguishes rule checkers from simple linting tools is the ability to analyze the design as a whole and to apply the relevant rules across the hierarchy. This capability is essential in checking hardware description languages because the actual problem may cross several hierarchical boundaries and involve a number of the design modules. A typical example of this is a combinational feedback path which has resulted from incorrectly connecting a module or group of modules at a higher level in the hierarchy.

Figure 2-3 contains examples of hierarchical rules from a commercially available rule checker. In order to apply these hierarchical rules the design needs to be built in some way. This is often referred to as elaboration or flattening the hierarchy. This process can be expensive in terms of run time and computer memory. VN-Check™ from TransEDA® uses a 'demand-driven' synthesis technique to minimize the impact of applying hierarchical rules.

Rule Name	Rule Description
ModuleHierarchyLevels	Limiting the levels of hierarchy in modules will produce easily readable and maintainable code
InternallyGeneratedClocks	Avoiding internally generated clocks and requiring that a clock be a simple port in the module simplifies design and analysis.
InternallyGeneratedPresets	Avoiding internally generated presets and requiring that a preset be a simple port in the module simplifies design and analysis.
InternallyGeneratedResets	Avoiding internally generated resets and requiring that a reset be a simple port in the module simplifies design and analysis.
OneTopLevelModule	This rule can be used to ensure that there is only one top-level module in the entire design.
CombinationalFeedbackLoops	This rule checks for local and hierarchical combinational feedback loops.

Figure 2-3

Each rule can have a value or attribute attached to it that defines how the rule will be used and what degree of checking is to be applied. For example an attribute could be a two-way switch which is used to indicate whether the particular requirement that the rule is checking for is allowed/disallowed or required/not required in the HDL code. Checking which edge of a clock is the active edge is another example of how attributes could be used. In this situation all clock signals could be checked to ensure that the same clock edge is used (all positive or all negative) or that clock edges are consistent across the whole design. Numerical quantities or text strings could also be used as attributes to define the value and type of check a rule should perform.

To see how rules can be configured to match a company's code of practice consider the following guidelines that designers in a particular company should adhere to.

- Each 'case' construct must contain a default clause.

- No more than 8 'case' items can appear in any 'case' construct.

- To improve readability 'tab' characters are not allowed in the source code.

- The length of each line of source code is limited to 72 characters.

- Only one HDL statement should appear on a line.

- All clock signals must begin with the prefix 'clk'.

Listed below is a typical group of rules that will check for the above situation.

```
rule_name=CaseDefault              value=Required
rule_name=CaseItems                value=8
rule_name=TabsInSource             value=Disallow
rule_name=LineLength               value=72
rule_name=SingleStatementPerLine   value=Required
rule_name=ClockNamePrefix          value=clk
```

After the relevant rules have been chosen and set up, the next step is to run the various HDL source code files through the rule-based checker and see which rules have been violated. This step normally involves inspecting the diagnostic and error reports produced by the rule-based checker to determine which line(s) of code contain errors and what actions are required to fix the problem(s). The modified HDL source files are then re-run through the rule-based checker. This iterative process is repeated until all errors have been fixed or the reasons for any outstanding errors have been explained and accepted by the designer.

Figure 2-4 shows the sequence that is normally used to select the rule databases and HDL design files prior to running the rule-based checker.

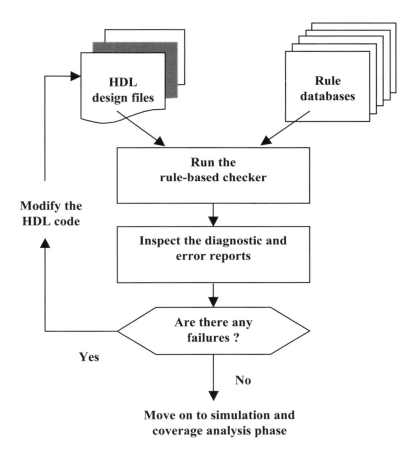

Figure 2-4

Appendix-B contains some practical examples of how a commercial rule-based checker can be used to check a set of HDL source files.

The actual rule-based checker used in Appendix-B is VN-Check™. This is a configurable rule-based checker that is available from TransEDA® as an optional module in their verification environment known as Verification Navigator®.

This page is intentionally left blank.

Chapter 3

Introduction to Coverage Analysis

THE ORIGINS OF COVERAGE ANALYSIS

Coverage analysis was originally developed at the time when third generation software languages like Pascal, ADA and C started to appear in the 1980s. These languages were fundamentally different to previous languages like BASIC in that they were structured and required the programmer to be much more organised and disciplined. For example, before a variable could be used it had to be declared together with the type of information (i.e. bit, binary, string, integer or floating) that it would be handling. Placing this simple discipline on the programmer enabled the software compiler to check and trap situations where the program tried to write the wrong type of information to a variable. Although this facility was useful, it only solved part of the problem because type checking was restricted to checking data and it did not help uncover problems associated with the logical behavior of the program. The emphasis was on checking the data rather than the control logic. For example, the reason why a program gets stuck in an infinite loop might just be that a particular variable is not incremented and therefore fails to satisfy a logical or arithmetic test at some point later in the program. Finding this type of logical design error can be time consuming, especially if the program contains hundreds of lines of code rather than small self-contained procedures or functions.

The first generation of coverage analysis tools were fairly rudimentary and did no more than simply report the current state of the variables used in the program and the lines of code that had been executed. Coverage analysis techniques became more sophisticated as they started to address the problems associated with the control flow of a program as well as the data. For example, the values of the variables that were used in conditional statements like 'if' and 'case' constructs could be tracked so that the programmer could see why a particular branch had or had not been taken.

Consider the following line of code:

```
if carry==1 or line_count>=80 then
```

Using coverage analysis techniques a programmer could find out whether the branch was taken because:

- carry was true and line_count was never true,

- line_count was true and carry was never true,

- carry and line_count were true at least once during the execution of the computer program.

The use of coverage analysis techniques gained momentum as programmers quickly realized that they could improve their levels of productivity and the quality of their programs by adopting these tools. Finding innovative methods of testing software continues to be a critical factor, as the size of computer programs tends to increase as the size of memory devices increase and the unit cost of storage falls. This means that coverage analysis techniques need to be applied at the subroutine, procedure or function level as well as the system programming level.

APPLYING COVERAGE ANALYSIS TECHNIQUES TO HDL

Because the two HDLs (hardware description languages) Verilog and VHDL are fundamentally very similar to other structured languages it was a natural progression to apply coverage analysis techniques to these tools. In fact the syntax and structure of Verilog is based very closely on the 'C' language whilst the origins of VHDL can be traced to Pascal and ADA.

By applying coverage analysis techniques to hardware description languages productivity was improved by enabling a designer to isolate areas of un-tested or inadequately covered HDL code. As every piece of un-tested code can potentially contain a coding error it can be seen that it is extremely important to identify these areas and exercise them with an appropriate set of test vectors. In this way a designer can quickly build confidence in the 'correctness' of the design and show that it meets the original specification before committing excessive amounts of time and money to further development of the product.

MODERN HARDWARE DESIGN TOOLS

During the last ten years there have been a significant number of changes that have affected how products that contain hardware and software are designed in the majority of companies today. Perhaps the most fundamental change that has occurred is the introduction of hardware description languages and logic synthesis tools, although the increase in the power and sophistication of logic simulators should not be overlooked. All of these changes have probably been dwarfed by the exponential increase that has occurred in the packing density of electronic circuits and the number of transistors that can be integrated onto a silicon chip. Today the limiting factor in electronic design is not *"Is there a chip that is large enough for my design?"* but *"Are there design tools with sufficient capacity to handle my design?"*

Instead of producing a hardware prototype a designer now has access to a HDL and a logic simulator that can be used to develop the product and prove that it operates correctly. At this stage the design could be completely abstract and bear little relationship to physical hardware. These modern development tools enable any number of iterative changes to be made to the design quickly and easily during the product design cycle. Once the product design operates correctly then the designer can move on and consider how the product should be implemented. Various factors may influence this step. For example, the physical size of the final product, manufacturing cost, customer perception of how the product should look, product marketing requirements, etc. This means that the design team have to make decisions to determine which parts of the product should be implemented in software and which parts will be implemented in hardware.

Translating the design from the HDL level into physical hardware is normally carried out automatically using a synthesis tool or may be done manually if the design is very small. As well as saving a considerable amount of time and effort, synthesis tools also enable a designer to target different types, sizes and speeds of FPGAs, and by applying a number of 'what if' decisions find the most cost-effective solution for the product.

Many designers consider synthesis to be a milestone event in a product development cycle. This is because any changes that are introduced from this point onwards are costly in terms of time and money. It can also involve a lengthy iterative loop if changes need to be made to the original HDL code because re-simulation and re-synthesis will need to be performed. Showing that the design is functionally correct before the synthesis stage is reached is a goal that all designers aim to achieve.

Selecting the most appropriate coverage analysis tool for a particular project can obviously help to achieve the goals outlined above as well as providing the designer with a high degree of confidence that the design is functionally correct.

TYPICAL CAPABILITIES OF COVERAGE ANALYSIS TOOLS

The coverage analysis tools that are currently available can be divided into two main groups. There are the tools developed by independent software tool suppliers and those developed by logic simulator vendors. Which tool you should use depends on a number of factors, some of which are listed below.

- Is more than one HDL used within your organisation?

Some organisations, particularly multi-national companies, may use Verilog in one division and VHDL in another and share HDL code between project groups. If this is the case then you may want to consider using a coverage analysis tool that can support both HDLs. Some coverage analysis tools offer just single language support while others offer language neutral or dual language capabilities. Choose the tool that matches the current and future needs of your organisation.

- Is more than one type of simulator used within your organisation?

Again some companies have standardised on the type of simulator that is used throughout the organisation while others may use Verilog in one division and VHDL in another. This means that you need to ensure that the coverage analysis tool you select will satisfy the needs of all your designers.

- What are your coverage analysis needs?

The number and type of coverage analysis measurements can vary dramatically between tool vendors. Although statement and branch coverage is offered by most of the vendors, one or two of the tool suppliers offer a rich set of measurements that are particularly useful when tackling control or data problems at the sub-system and system integration level. Detailed descriptions of various coverage analysis measurements appear in Chapter 6 of this manual.

HOW COVERAGE ANALYSIS TOOLS OPERATE

The remaining part of this chapter will take a brief look at how a typical coverage analysis tool is used to extract and present information to a HDL designer or verification engineer. A coverage analysis tool performs three basic functions:

- Analyzing the HDL source code

- Collecting coverage data from the simulation

- Presenting the results to the user

Analyzing the HDL source code

During this phase the coverage analysis tool inspects the HDL source code to determine where monitor points known as *probes* should be inserted in order to collect the maximum amount of information about simulation activity in the design. It is crucial that the source code is not altered in any way, so this process (known as *instrumenting*) must be non-intrusive and is normally carried out by making copies of the original source files and instrumenting those files. Different types of probes are used depending on the type of coverage measurements selected by the user.

A set of control files is also created at the analysis stage. These files are used to define the maximum number of possible ways the code can be executed. For example, a simple two way branch for an `if` statement will have the value 2 stored in the control file, while a `case` construct with say six different decision paths will have the value 6 stored. At this stage the mappings to a designer's work area and component libraries will also be set up if any VHDL code is used in the design.

Collecting coverage data from the simulation

Most coverage analysis tools automatically invoke the appropriate logic simulator (i.e. Verilog or VHDL) and run a normal simulation to collect information about activity in the design. The information collected from the various probes that were embedded in the source files is used to build a series of history files for each design unit or module in the design. The information in the history file defines what actually happened during the simulation. When this figure is compared with the values in the corresponding control files it enables the percentage coverage to be computed. An example of how branch coverage is calculated for a `Case` construct is given below.

```
Branch coverage=(Case_History/Case_Control)*100
```

where `Case_History` is the number of actual branches taken and `Case_Control` is the maximum number of branches that could have been taken.

In a number of situations all a designer or verification engineer really wants to know is that a certain piece of HDL code has been exercised a minimum number of times. For example in a multi-way branch all that may be required, during the early stages of verification, is knowing that every branch has been taken. So the absolute number of times each branch has been taken may not be so important. Some coverage analysis tools have sophisticated probe management facilities that enable a probe to be automatically deactivated once it has collected a predefined amount of information. This mechanism can help reduce the simulation overhead when many changes are performed to the HDL code during the early phases of the project development.

Presenting the results to the user

The previous two stages have analyzed the HDL code and collected the results from the logic simulation. The last phase is to present the results to the user in such a way that the problem areas can be highlighted quickly so that effort can be directed accordingly.

One of the traps that a user can easily fall into is collecting too much information. Then more time is spent wading through the results searching for where the problems are located than fixing the problems. The temptation is to switch on all the different coverage measurements for the whole of the design just so that you do not miss anything! A better methodology, which will be described in greater detail later, is to partition the design into functional blocks, single design units or modules and to apply appropriate coverage measurements. This means initially starting with statement and branch coverage to find the obvious and simple coding problems, and then moving on to the more powerful measurements to find the obscure and difficult problems.

Most coverage analysis tools enable the results to be displayed graphically on the screen as well as generating textual printouts. Hierarchical views, color-coding and filtering techniques are all used to enable a user to quickly navigate to the problem areas. A selection of these techniques is described in detail in Chapter 6 of this manual together with screen shots that give examples of how this information is conveyed to a user.

COMMAND LINE AND BATCH MODE

Most coverage analysis tools include a command line interface that enables a user to drive the tools directly from the keyboard, a script or a batch file. This facility is especially useful in projects where there may be hundreds of HDL source files that need to be instrumented and simulated before the coverage results can be inspected.

Some form of automation, using a batch file, is also imperative when the regression test suite is run after changes are made to an HDL source file. More information on analyzing and optimizing the test suite can be found in Chapter 12 of this manual.

Chapter 4

Coverage Analysis in the Design Flow

CURRENT ASIC DESIGN FLOW

The modern ASIC design flow has evolved and increased in complexity just as the devices that are being designed have dramatically increased in complexity. This design flow is now heavily dependent on EDA tools and many of the tasks that were once carried out manually are now automated by EDA tools with little or no manual intervention.

As a function of this increase in complexity it has been necessary for designers and verification engineers to seek out higher levels of abstraction to carry out their respective tasks.

This abstraction of the design process means that designers develop their designs in hardware description languages such as Verilog and VHDL. These languages not only allow designers to describe logic gates; they can also specify abstract types, such as the states of a state machine, and complex operations, such as multiply, in a single line of HDL code.

So powerful are these hardware description languages that two levels of abstraction in the design flow are now possible; namely, RTL (Register Transfer Level) and Behavioral level.

The design flow including these two levels of abstraction is shown in Figure 4-1.

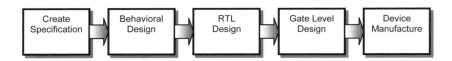

Figure 4-1

As with all design projects the flow starts with a specification. Currently there is no universally accepted way of capturing a specification. Usually it is a complex written document that immediately runs the risk of containing ambiguities. It is for this reason that many large design companies employ two teams - a design team and verification team both working from the same specification. The idea here is that any ambiguities are trapped using this two-pronged attack.

From the specification a behavioral description of the design is generated. Currently this process has to be done manually. Normally the behavioral description is captured in a hardware description language such as VHDL or Verilog or even C++. Once the behavioral description has been captured the designer has a formal unambiguous circuit description that can be executed and therefore tested against the specification. This is an important stage in the process because already at this early stage the design can be tested for misconceptions. Bringing in verification as early as possible is critical in the modern design process because the process is so long sometimes months or even years and discovering a major conceptual error late in the design process would result in significant time and cost over-runs. Whether using VHDL or Verilog - or a combination of both languages, verification is usually carried out using one of the many commercially available HDL simulators.

The design is tested by applying a number of stimuli, test vectors or test benches - usually written in the same language as the design - and checking the resulting responses. This may be done either manually or automatically if the simulator allows it and if the expected responses are included in what is then known as a self-checking test bench.

Having verified the behavioral design the next step in the process is to decompose this to an RTL description. While RTL is still a level of abstraction above gate level, the design blocks, combinational logic and registers can be clearly identified. In fact 80% of a design's structure is typically fixed at the RTL stage. Transforming a design from a behavioral description into RTL is still a largely manual process. Most of the functional verification (in terms of time spent) is done at the RTL stage. HDL simulation is the most frequently used functional verification technique - most designers and verification engineers having access to at least one simulator. The RTL design process is potentially the most significant task in the design process and is therefore usually further subdivided as shown in Figure 4-2.

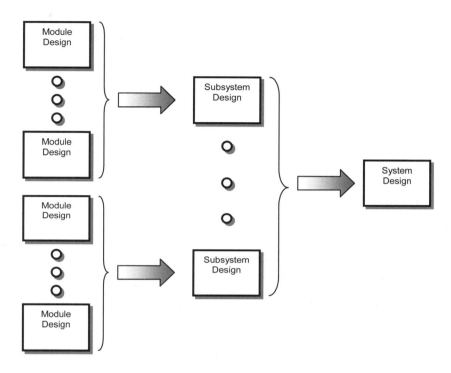

Figure 4-2

The first step is to divide the functionality into a number of blocks, modules or design units. Once these modules have been developed and tested they are merged into subsystems and then the functionality of these items is verified. Finally the subsystems are integrated into the full system and it is verified. By subdividing the problem more development engineers can work in parallel to reduce the overall project time.

After completing the RTL design the next step is to transform this description into a gate level description in the target ASIC technology. This process is known as logic synthesis and is now predominantly a fully automatic process, with more than one software package available in the market today. Again the functionality of the system is verified at gate level although this process usually involves using timing data from automatic place and route tools to make the simulations as accurate as possible. The purpose of the verification at this stage is to determine that the system operates correctly with the timing constraints of the physical ASIC device. Gate level simulations take significantly longer than RTL simulations.

The other operation that is performed on the gate level description is *Fault Simulation*. The purpose of this is to create a set of tests which will be used to verify the actual ASIC is free from production defects once it has been manufactured. These tests can bare little relationship to the functionality of the device. Fault simulations take much greater simulation effort than normal functional simulations.

The final stage in the process, once the physical layout has been completed, is to manufacture the actual devices, after which the tests created by fault simulation can be run to verify the manufacturing process.

COVERAGE ANALYSIS IN THE DESIGN FLOW

Coverage analysis identifies the parts of your HDL code that are executed during simulation and, more importantly, highlights the parts of the code that have *not* been executed. You may think that it is obvious to a designer what has been tested, but this is very often not the case. The problem is made far worse when there are separate design and verification teams working on the same project. Figure 4-3 shows the problem graphically. Initially the amount of HDL code tested increases rapidly but, as the verification process continues, the rate at which HDL code is covered decreases until finally it is very difficult to determine whether all the HDL code has been executed.

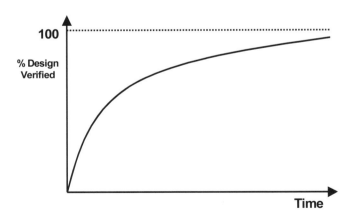

Figure 4-3

This uncertainty of what has been executed is a big risk to the project. Any code that has not been tested may contain errors and the effect of these errors is completely unknown. Should one of these errors be found later in the project, for example during gate level simulation, or after the device has been manufactured the cost of fixing the problem is much greater - as indicated in Figure 4-4. Not only is the cost a problem, but the project time-scales could be seriously compromised and the company could miss the window of opportunity for the product.

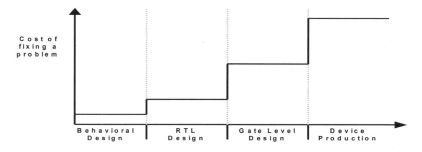

Figure 4-4

Figure 4-5 shows the effect of applying coverage analysis to the project. Each simulation that is run with coverage analysis shows the areas of the design that have not yet been tested so that the next batch of tests can target the untested functionality. This coverage directed verification process gives the design and verification team much greater confidence that their design has been 100% tested. In addition coverage directed verification means that less time is wasted re-testing parts of the design that have already been covered and more time is spent on targeting the untested areas of the design.

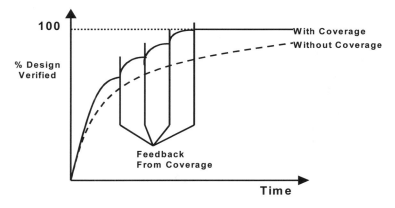

Figure 4-5

Coverage analysis not only helps with the verification process. It also helps with planning and time-scale estimation. Coverage analysis gives continuous feedback on what proportion of the design is left to be verified and, based on the time taken so far, an accurate estimate of how much time is required to complete the testing.

There are number of coverage analysis tools for Verilog available today. One of the most comprehensive and well established of these is Verification Navigator from TransEDA. Verification Navigator is also the only true VHDL coverage analysis tool on the market.

There are three occasions during the design flow described earlier where the functionality of the design is verified. These are at the behavioral level, at the RTL level and at the gate level. However, because 80% of the design structure is set at the RTL stage, and RTL design is carried out using either VHDL or Verilog, it is the RTL level that is the most suitable stage for using coverage analysis.

RTL design comprises three basic parts 1) module design, 2) subsystem integration 3) system integration as shown in Figure 4-6. Verification is carried out at all three of these stages and therefore it is appropriate to use coverage analysis at each of these stages. By ensuring that a module is thoroughly verified before it is integrated into the rest of the design, the risk of finding a problem later in the design cycle is significantly reduced. It is also much easier to test individual blocks than a complete system.

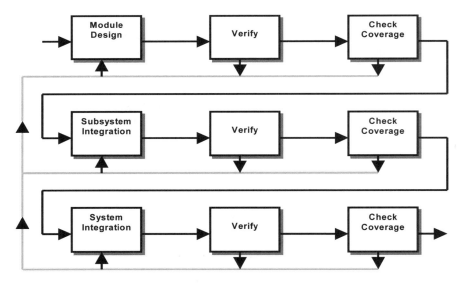

Figure 4-6

Coverage analysis is still applicable once the modules have been integrated together to form subsystems and systems to ensure that the glue logic that joins the modules is fully tested and that all possible operations of the module have been tested within the bounds of the system.

Coverage analysis does not need to be used only at the RTL stage; behavioral design is also often done using VHDL and Verilog and it is just as important to ensure the behavioral level design is fully executed. Fully testing the behavioral design ensures that all the design concepts have been fully explored.

Gate level descriptions can be expressed as Verilog or VHDL netlists. These netlists, however, do not contain any of the constructs that are usually tested with coverage analysis. In fact the only things that can be examined at gate level are the signals in the design. This does not mean that coverage analysis is a waste of time at gate level because Verification Navigator and a few of the other coverage analysis tools can perform a check known as Toggle Coverage. Toggle coverage is useful as a measure of the amount of data applied to gate level descriptions and as a pre-cursor to fault simulation.

Figure 4-7 shows the design flow described above.

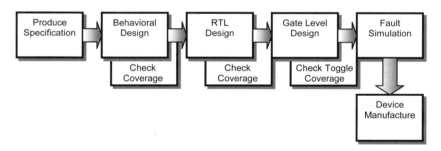

Figure 4-7

IP IN THE DESIGN FLOW

Modern designs have become so large that a single device can be a whole system on a chip (SoC). It is for this reason that many chip design teams now use IP (intellectual property). These are cores of functionality which have been already written in a HDL and can be easily included in a design. IP cores can be devices that were once large ICs; for example - the Pentium processor. The idea behind using IP blocks is to save on design effort. In actual fact the cost of using an IP block is between 30% and 100% of the time to design the block from scratch depending on the quality of the IP core. IP blocks are always written in RTL so that they can be synthesized. Figure 4-8 shows the design flow including IP blocks.

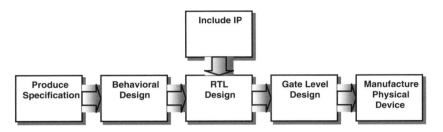

Figure 4-8

When employing an IP block it is essential to know the quality of the test benches that accompany that block. It is for this reason that coverage analysis should be used on the IP block, just as it would be used on a block developed as part of the project.

In addition, it is essential to continue to apply coverage analysis to the IP block when it has been integrated into the design, in order to verify that the interface to the IP block has been fully tested and that all aspects of the block's behavior have been tested within the bounds of your system. Figure 4-9 shows the process of IP integration including verification with coverage analysis.

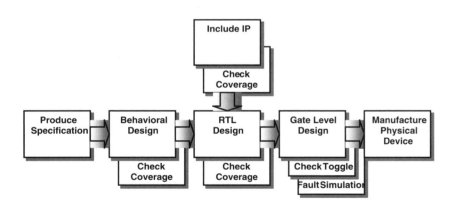

Figure 4-9

Today's ASIC design flow is a long and complex process because of the size and sophistication of the devices being produced. It is for this reason that it is critical that the devices are 'right first time'. If they are not, a failure in the field is not only costly but it is technologically embarrassing and is likely to also be financially detrimental. In addition, the window of opportunity can be missed and market share lost -

sometimes irrecoverably. It pays to ensure that the products that are released will meet the customers' expectations - which means that extensive verification must be carried out. Major semiconductor manufacturers now realise this and that is why, in many companies, design verification can account for up to 70% of the total cost of the entire design process.

Because of the relative cost, any tool that makes this verification process more reliable and shorter has to be a 'must have'. The feedback that coverage analysis produces is invaluable in making the verification process more reliable, timescales more predictable and generally aiding the whole process.

This page is intentionally left blank.

Chapter 5

Practical Value of Coverage Analysis

HDL VERIFICATION PROBLEM

Testing proves the existence of bugs in a design; it does not prove their absence. The only way to ensure that a design is bug free is to fully test the whole design. This sounds like a simple enough concept. However in reality today's designs are so large and complex it is not an easy task to ensure the design is fully verified. Over the last four years the verification portion of the design process has increased significantly, from about 30% - 40% to 50% - 80%, as shown in Figure 5-1. This makes verification the most significant part of the ASIC development process.

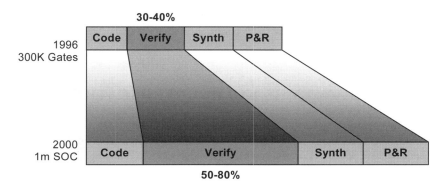

Figure 5-1

The problem is made worse by the competitive environment that exists today. Project time scales have to be met to avoid being beaten onto the market by the competition.

Figure 5-2 shows how the rate of bugs found decreases as a typical verification project proceeds. Initially the rate at which bugs are found is high. As the design matures the rate decreases. The problem is deciding when to ship the design.

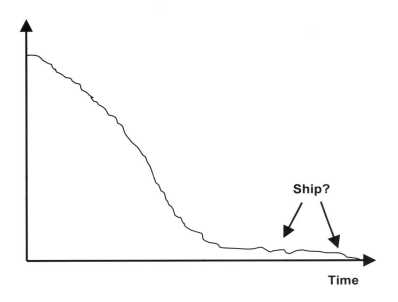

Figure 5-2

Each fix introduces the risk of adding new bugs and any yet untested code could also still contain bugs. The only way to be confident that it is safe to ship your design is to ensure it is fully tested.

COVERAGE ANALYSIS AND HDL VERIFICATION

During the behavioral and RTL design phases of a project HDL coverage analysis tools such as Verification Navigator from TransEDA can be used to measure the amount of Verilog or VHDL code which has been executed during simulation.

Using coverage analysis to direct your verification process gives you a big advantage. Coverage analysis highlights the parts of your design that have not yet been executed, and therefore may contain bugs. Using this information you can concentrate your verification effort on the untested parts of your design.

Figure 5-3 shows the typical effect of using coverage analysis on the rate of bug detection in the verification process.

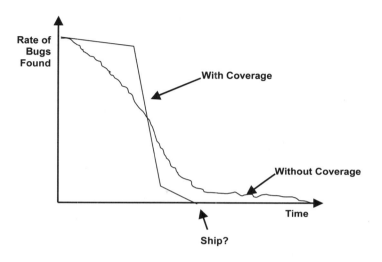

Figure 5-3

Using coverage directed verification the rate at which the bugs are found remains higher for longer. However it then decreases rapidly as the amount of HDL code executed approaches 100% and the bug rate drops to zero more quickly than without using coverage analysis. This demonstrates the value of coverage analysis in improving the verification process.

PROJECT MANAGEMENT WITH COVERAGE ANALYSIS

Coverage analysis not only helps to detect bugs but can also be used to help with project planning. The detailed information that most coverage analysis tools produce show exactly what proportion of the design is still to be verified. This information can then be used to make accurate predictions of when the verification process will be completed.

Quality control departments also benefit from the coverage analysis reports. These reports give documentary evidence of verification quality. Some companies already make coverage analysis a mandatory requirement in their design flow.

FUNCTIONAL COVERAGE

Coverage analysis does not prove that a design is functionally correct. It is still important and necessary to check the simulation results. The best way to do this is with a self checking test bench, which verifies the outputs of the design are correct for specific inputs. There is a correlation between functional coverage. However the size of the correlation depends on the amount of coverage measurements your tool provides and the number you use to test your design. Consider the statement below.

```
a <= b * c;
```

If this statement is tested with b=0 and c=0 you will have covered the line, but you would get the same simulation result if the operation was multiply, add, logical-and or logical-or, so the functionality has not been covered (verified). If extra measurements are used to ensure a range of values are passed through b and c you can be confident that the functionality of this example line has been fully covered.

REGRESSION TESTING

Coverage analysis can be used as criteria for regression test suite selection. In most cases the test suite for a design will cover the same code over and over again. From a coverage analysis point of view some of these tests are redundant. This situation is very common when using pseudo random test generation. The results of coverage analysis can be used to identify those tests that do not improve the coverage. These 'redundant' tests could be omitted for short regression suites for example nightly or weekly runs. By sorting your test runs in this way you can ensure the maximum amount of your HDL code is tested by the regression tests. It also ensures the regression suite is short enough to be executed in the time available, for example overnight. The amount of redundancy in a regression suite varies greatly from company to company and design-to-design. Reductions of 10:1 are possible and have been achieved. The sorting of tests can be made more sophisticated by using different coverage criteria for different levels of regression testing. Nightly regression suites, for example, could be selected using the most basic coverage analysis measurements. Weekly suites could be selected using the rest of the coverage measurements and the remaining tests could be added for the monthly regression suite.

With most coverage analysis tools this regression suite sorting would have to be done manually or with scripts written by the user, however Verification Navigator from TransEDA has this regression suite ordering capability built in.

GATE LEVEL TESTING

At gate level the design is purely structural so the use of coverage analysis tools is limited. Only those coverage tools that provide toggle coverage such as Verification Navigator from TransEDA give any benefit at this stage. Toggle coverage is a check to see if the tests can apply both 0 and 1 value on all the signals in the design.

At gate level, however, toggle coverage has another important use in that it can be used as a pre-cursor to gate level fault simulation which is performed to generate tests to check the manufactured device.

Effective fault simulation relies on two circuit parameters, namely, Controllability and Observability. Controllability tests whether a 0 and a 1 can be applied to each node in the circuit, Observability checks whether the effect of a fault on each node in the circuit can be observed at the output pins.

A high value for controllability is critical for good fault simulation results and because there is a 100% correlation between toggle coverage and controllability, a high value for toggle coverage is necessary for good fault simulation results. But, because toggle coverage is run on the normal functional simulation, it is *much* faster than fault simulation and therefore more efficient than using fault simulation from the outset.

This page is intentionally left blank.

Chapter 6

Coverage Analysis Measurements

This chapter provides a detailed description of the coverage analysis measurements that can be applied to the development and testing of high quality HDL code. The measurements described are:

- Statement coverage

- Branch coverage

- Condition and expression coverage

- Path coverage

- Toggle coverage

- Triggering coverage

- Signal-tracing coverage

It should be noted that the term 'coverage metrics' is often used by design engineers to refer to the overall set of coverage analysis measurements mentioned above. It should also be noted that there are a number of coverage analysis tools available in the EDA marketplace that operate on various platforms from personal computers to high-end workstations. Although some of these tools have more coverage measurements than others, Verification Navigator (from TransEDA) has the richest set of coverage metrics and as such will be used for the majority of examples referred to in this chapter. Please note that tools from different vendors may use slightly different terminology to refer to the same coverage analysis measurements. For example, statement and branch coverage is quite often referred to as block coverage.

Coverage metrics can be classified according to the benefit that they offer to a designer and whether the testing strategy is being applied at the structural or functional level.

STRUCTURAL AND FUNCTIONAL TESTING

Structural testing, also known as white box or open box testing, is normally applied to sequential HDL code and concentrates on checking that all executable statements within each module have been exercised and the corresponding branches and paths through that module have been covered. If there is a section of HDL code that has never been exercised then there is a high possibility that it could contain an error that will remain undetected. One of the objectives of structural testing is to raise the designer's confidence level that the HDL code does not contain any untested areas and behaves in a manner that closely matches the original design specification. Structural testing can therefore be considered as concentrating on checking that the control logic operates correctly. The coverage measurements that fall into this category are: statement, branch, condition and expression, and path coverage.

Functional testing, also known as black box or closed box testing, is normally applied to HDL code that operates concurrently and concentrates on checking the interaction between modules, blocks or functional boundaries. The objective here is to ensure that 'correct results' are obtained when 'good inputs' are applied to the various parts of the design, and when 'bad inputs' are applied the design operates in a predictable manner. Functional testing can therefore be considered as concentrating on checking that the data paths operate correctly. The coverage measurements that fall into this category are: toggle, triggering, and signal trace coverage.

STATEMENT COVERAGE

Although statement coverage is the least powerful of all the coverage metrics it is probably the easiest to understand and use. It gives a very quick overview of which parts of the design have failed to achieve 100% coverage and where extra verification effort is needed. Statement coverage is applied to signal and variable assignments in HDL code and gives an indication of the number of times each assignment statement was executed when the design was simulated. A zero execution count pin-points a line of code that has not been exercised that could be the source of a potential design error. The following example shows a line of code that has not been exercised and how this fact could be indicated to a designer using a coverage analysis tool.

```
Execution count       HDL code
***0***               NewColor <= '1';        (VHDL)
***0***               NewColor = 1;           (Verilog)
```

Color-coding and error navigation buttons are used by many coverage analysis tools to assist the designer in quickly locating lines of code with zero execution counts. Figure 6-1 shows an example of how zero statement coverage is reported graphically in Verification Navigator.

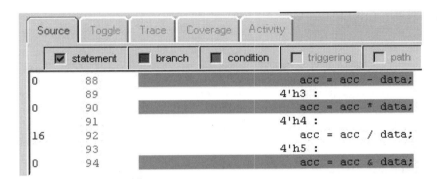

Figure 6-1

The figures in the left-hand column of Figure 6-1 indicate the execution count for each statement. The next column gives the line number reference to the HDL source code. Color-coding is used to highlight lines where there are zero execution counts, such as lines 88, 90 and 94 in Figure 6-1.

Statement coverage is also useful in identifying exceedingly high execution counts that could cause potential bottlenecks during the simulation phase or could indicate sections of HDL code that would benefit from being re-written using a more efficient coding style. An example of how high execution counts are displayed in Verification Navigator is shown in Figure 6-2.

```
  Source   Toggle   Trace   Coverage   Activity

  ☑ statement   ■ branch   ■ condition   ☐ triggering   ☐ path

              133       begin
1001          134          ctrl1 = clk ? ir[15] && ir[14] :   0;
1001          135          ctrl2 = (!clk || &ir[15:12])  && rst;
1001          136          ctrl3 = (ir[15] || ir[14])  && rst;
              137          if (ctrl1 && ctrl2 && ctrl3)
              138          begin
16            139             ctrl1 = 0;
```

Figure 6-2

Statement coverage problems do not normally occur in isolation, they are usually associated with some other failure within the HDL code. For example, if a branch through a particular piece of code is never taken for some reason, then all the executable statements within that branch will be identified with a zero execution count marker.

If, in Figure 6-3, `a` always equals `b` then statement coverage will be 50% because the block of statements in the FALSE path are never taken.

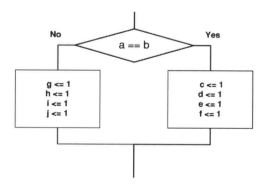

Figure 6-3

It is advisable to aim for 100% statement coverage before using other, more powerful, coverage metrics.

BRANCH COVERAGE

Branch coverage is invaluable to the designer as it offers diagnostics as to why certain sections of HDL code, containing zero or more assignment statements, were not executed. This coverage metric measures how many times each branch in an IF or CASE construct was executed and is particularly useful in situations where a branch does not contain any executable statements. For example, the ELSE branch in an IF statement may be missing or empty, or may contain further nested branching constructs. Quite often, during the development phase of a design, a test bench may be incomplete and may focus on exercising the normal control paths through the module rather than the exceptions. Branch coverage is essential in this situation, as it shows immediately which branches have not been tested.

The example given in Figure 6-4 shows that if 'b' always equals 'a' then statement coverage will be 100% but branch coverage will only be 50% and the empty ELSE branch is never taken. Just like statement coverage, the aim should be to achieve 100% branch coverage before using other, more powerful, coverage metrics.

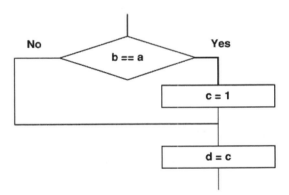

Figure 6-4

How Branch Coverage is Calculated

During the analysis phase the coverage analysis tool will work out the total number of possible branches that could be taken through the HDL code construct. This value is then compared against the number of branches that were actually taken and the result expressed as a percentage. Figure 6-5 shows that there are three possible branches through the construct and that the construct has been entered 52 times. Although Posedge Clk has been true and false, Reset has always been false which means that only two of the possible three paths through the construct have been taken. If this is expressed as a percentage it will equate to 66% branch coverage.

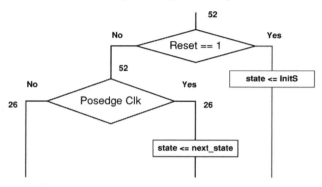

Figure 6-5

The examples described so far in this chapter use a single condition to control the branch statement. In this situation it is fairly obvious to see why a particular branch was taken or not taken. If the branch is controlled by a series of multiple conditions then it can become more difficult to determine which condition actually caused the branch to be taken. Most coverage analysis tools automatically provide further in-depth analysis for the designer when branches with multiple conditions are detected. This in-depth analysis is known as condition and expression coverage.

CONDITION AND EXPRESSION COVERAGE

Although statement and branch coverage provide an excellent indication of the coverage that has been achieved in a design, using condition and expression coverage can extend the usefulness of this information even further. Condition coverage measures that the test bench has tested all combinations of the sub-expressions that are used in complex branches. The following example shows a code fragment that has a complex condition associated with the branch statement.

```
Execution count        HDL pseudo code
12                     if (A = '1');
***0***                   if (B = '1' and C = '0') then
***0***                      D <= '1';
                          end if;
                       end if;
```

In the above example it can be seen that the execution count of zero for if (B=1 and C=0) requires additional test vectors in order to check the branching signals B and C. Using a coverage analysis tool, on this particular line of code, would reveal the actual

combinations of the signals B and C that had been exercised. A typical set of
condition coverage results for signals B and C is shown in the truth table below.

```
Execution count    B=1    C=0
9                   0      0      (i.e. B=0 and C=1)
***0***             0      1      (i.e. B=0 and C=0)
3                   1      0      (i.e. B=1 and C=1)
***0***             1      1      (i.e. B=1 and C=0)
```

The above truth table indicates that C=0 has never been true and that extra test
vectors are needed for this signal in order to achieve 100% condition coverage.

Most coverage analysis tools should have the capability to enable the results for
condition coverage to be displayed in various formats that match the needs of the
designer and hence improve overall design productivity.

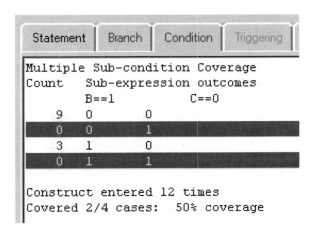

Figure 6-6

Multiple Sub-Condition Coverage

Multiple sub-condition coverage is probably the most popular analysis method. The
presentation format shows in an easy-to-read truth table layout all the possible
combinations associated with the execution of the branch statement. An example of
how multiple sub-condition coverage is presented by Verification Navigator is shown
in Figure 6-6.

Basic Sub-Condition Coverage

This analysis method checks that each term in the sub-expression has been both true and false during the simulation phase. Again it is fairly normal for the coverage results to be displayed in a tabular format or truth table layout. Consider the following line of pseudo HDL code.

```
if (A == 1) || (B == 1 && C == 1)
```
A typical set of output results for the above expression displayed in basic sub-condition format is shown below.

```
6            : A == 1      1
3            : A == 1      0
***0***      : B == 1      1
9            : B == 1      0
7            : C == 1      1
2            : C == 1      0
```
Each term, in the branch expression, is listed on separate lines together with a count of the number of times that term was true and false. Obviously an extra vector is required in the test bench to check the condition for when B is true.

Although basic sub-condition coverage is the simplest criteria to understand and use, it does not uncover possible coding errors in the logic where an AND function should have been used instead of an OR function or vice-versa. For example, if the two vector sets of (a==0, b==0) and (a==1, b==1) were used to test the two branch statements if (a || b) and if (a && b), then basic sub-condition coverage will indicate all combinations have been covered. This means that a logical coding error in the design would go un-noticed and may not get picked up until much later in the development phase. Multiple sub-condition coverage on the other hand would indicate a zero execution count for the missing vector sets of (a==0, b==1) and (a==1, b==0).

Directed or Focused Expression Coverage (FEC)

Some coverage analysis tools offer a directed or focused expression coverage facility that helps to identify the minimum set of test vectors needed to fully validate complex branch expressions. The idea behind focused expression coverage is very simple and is based on the fact that when a designer writes a Boolean expression, the expression is an equation with a number of inputs (signals or variables in the HDL description) combined with Boolean operators (AND, NAND, OR, NOR, NOT or EXOR). If a signal or variable is used as an input to an expression, then that input needs to control the output of the expression otherwise that input is redundant. Focused expression coverage requires that for each input there is a pair of test vectors between which only that input changes value and for which the output is true for one test and false for the other.

As an example consider the expression

```
f = a && b;
```

The test vectors which satisfy the focused expression coverage criteria for input `a` are (a = 0, b = 1) and (a = 1, b = 1). Likewise, the test vectors for input `b` are (a = 1, b = 0) and (a = 1, b = 1). Because the vectors (a = 1, b = 1) are common to both inputs the actual number of tests needed to fully validate the above expression is 3. Figure 6-7 shows the test patterns that would be required for an expression consisting of AND and OR operators.

out = a && b && c && d ... && z

Inputs					Output
a	b	c	d	z	out
0	1	1	1	1	0
1	0	1	1	1	0
1	1	0	1	1	0
1	1	1	0	1	0
....					
1	1	1	1	0	0
1	1	1	1	1	1

out = a || b || c || d ... || z

Inputs					Output
a	b	c	d	z	out
1	0	0	0	0	1
0	1	0	0	0	1
0	0	1	0	0	1
0	0	0	1	0	1
....					
0	0	0	0	1	1
0	0	0	0	0	0

Figure 6-7

Although the reduction in the number of test vectors (from 4 to 3) may not at first sight appear very significant, the productivity benefit becomes substantial as the number of input terms in the expression increase.

Figure 6-8 illustrates the dramatic reduction in the number of test vectors that are needed when the focused expression methodology is used. As many companies estimate that testing can account for 60%-70% of the total development effort on a project, any effort that can be trimmed in this area will have a positive effect on reducing time-scales and will make savings in the overall budget. Furthermore, testing quite often involves 'shaking out' a suitable set of test vectors that will adequately exercise the circuit and promote the designer's confidence that the design works correctly and meets specification. Adopting a test strategy that minimizes the number of required test vectors will be highly beneficial both in terms of the time and the effort allocated to the project. One of the simplest and most common testing strategies is the 'exhaustive test' where every conceivable pattern is applied to the design under test. This particular testing technique is fairly popular because it is quite easy for a designer to write a test program to cycle through all the input combinations. However, the shortcomings of this particular testing method soon become apparent when a simple logic circuit consisting of N-inputs (i.e. an expression consisting of N-terms) is examined. Clearly the number of test vectors that will be needed if the exhaustive testing strategy is adopted will be 2^N for an N-input circuit.

Inputs	2^N	N+1
8	256	9
16	65,536	17
24	16,777,216	25
36	$4.295 * 10^9$	37

Figure 6-8

Assuming that test vectors could be applied to the module under test every 100nS, then Figure 6-9 clearly shows that the exponential growth in testing time is unacceptable and that a more efficient method must be found and adopted in the testing arena.

Number of Inputs	Exhaustive Method		FEC Method	
	Tests	Time	Tests	Time
20	2^{20}	0.1 S	21	2 uS
30	2^{30}	100 S	31	3 uS
40	2^{40}	27 hrs	41	4 uS

Figure 6-9

Unfortunately, alternative testing techniques usually involve a fair amount of effort on the part of the verification engineer, developing a dedicated testing strategy and compiling a unique set of test vectors. The focused or directed expression coverage methodology, as implemented by TransEDA, concentrates on choosing the most effective test vectors without the need to use every possible combination of input pattern. For example, if the HDL code fragment if (B==1 and C==0) was simulated with an incomplete set of test vectors e.g. (B=0, C=1) and (B=1, C=1) the graphical output, as illustrated in Figure 6-10, would be produced.

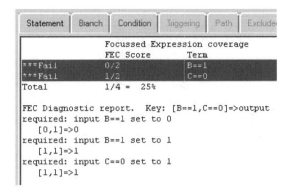

Statement	Branch	Condition	Triggering	Path	Exclude

```
                  Focussed Expression coverage
                  FEC Score          Term
***Fail           0/2                B==1
***Fail           1/2                C==0
Total             1/4 =   25%

FEC Diagnostic report.  Key: [B==1,C==0]=>output
required: input B==1 set to 0
   [0,1]=>0
required: input B==1 set to 1
   [1,1]=>1
required: input C==0 set to 1
   [1,1]=>1
```

Figure 6-10

The focused expression coverage score, as reported in the central column of Figure 6-10, shows that the term B==1 completely failed to control the branch and that term C==0 only achieved partial control, as only one correct vector out of a possible two vectors satisfied the FEC criteria. The usefulness of this particular methodology is enhanced by the inclusion of a diagnostic report that identifies missing vectors. In this case the missing vectors are (B=0, C=0) and (B=1, C=0). It is a relatively easy task for a verification engineer to add the missing test vectors to the test bench, thereby achieving 100% condition coverage for this particular branch statement.

PATH COVERAGE

If one complete branching statement follows another branching statement in a sequential block of HDL code, then a series of paths can occur between the blocks. The branching statement can be an IF or a CASE statement or any mixture of the two. Path coverage calculates how many combinations of branches in the first construct and branches in the second construct could be entered. It then measures how many of these combinations were actually executed during the simulation phase and expresses the result as a percentage. As an example, consider the two consecutive IF constructs shown in Figure 6-11. Although there are 4 paths through the complete construct and every branch has been taken at least once, it is not clear whether all the paths have actually been taken.

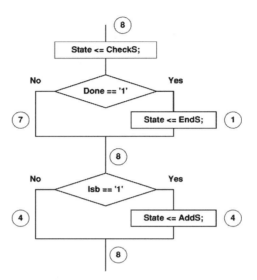

Figure 6-11

Figure 6-12 shows, using a flowchart format for illustration purposes, how the path coverage metric would measure the outcome of the decision for each branch and uses this information to identify paths that have a count of zero.

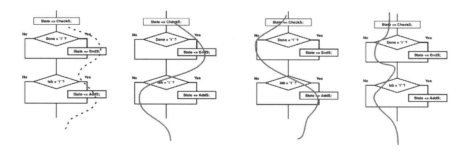

Figure 6-12

The listing below shows a possible way for a coverage analysis tool to show the path analysis results for a piece of HDL code that contains two consecutive decision statements at line numbers 38 and 41. It is normal practice to exclude assignment statements from the report in an effort to improve clarity.

```
0   38   IF Done =  '1'  THEN
    41   IF lsb  =  '1'  THEN
1   38   IF Done =  '1'  THEN
    43   All false condition for IF lsb = '1' THEN
4   40   All false condition for IF Done = '1' THEN
    41   IF lsb  =  '1'  THEN
3   40   All false condition for IF Done = '1' THEN
    43   All false condition for IF lsb = '1' THEN
```

The first column shows the execution count while the second column gives the line number of the HDL source code, which can be used for reference purposes. Combining the results in this way gives a very compact overview of which paths require further effort from the verification engineer. Another example showing the importance of path coverage is given in Figure 6-13. In this example it is assumed that the circuit design has been exercised with the test vectors (a=1, b=1) and (a=0, b=0). A verification engineer may be justifiably pleased with the results that showed that 100% statement and branch coverage was achieved, and then get alarmed when it is discovered that only 50% path coverage was achieved. In this particular example the path that assigns operand=0.0 (in the first IF statement) and result=1.0/operand (in the second IF statement) never gets executed. This means that the potentially dangerous calculation of 1/0.0 never occurs.

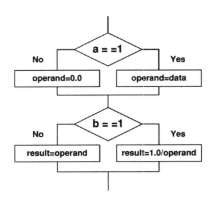

Figure 6-13

Although a designer should aim for 100% path coverage, in reality this may be difficult or impossible to achieve so a more realistic target may be 85% coverage. For example, if the variable assignments in the first or upper branch are not related to the second or lower branch then there is no reason to check path coverage through this particular construct.

TOGGLE COVERAGE

Toggle coverage has a slightly different terminology and interpretation depending on whether the Verilog or VHDL hardware description language is being used. If Verilog is being used then toggle coverage is known as variable toggle coverage and checks that each bit in the registers and nets of a module change polarity (i.e. 'toggles') and are not stuck at one particular level. If, on the other hand, VHDL is being used as the design language then toggle coverage is know as signal toggle coverage and evaluates the level of activity for each bit of every signal in the architecture. For a full toggle, a bit must change state, for example `0->1` and then change back again from `1->0`.

Toggle coverage is a very useful coverage measurement as it shows the amount of activity within the design and helps to pinpoint areas that have not been adequately verified by the test bench. It can be applied to structural or white box testing to prove that the control logic of the design is functioning correctly, and also to functional or black box testing to prove that signals that cross module boundaries are toggling adequately. The listing below shows a possible way for a coverage analysis tool to show the toggle coverage for a piece of HDL code that contains a register.

```
Count          Bit      Transition
***0***        aa[0]    posedge
***0***        aa[0]    negedge
1              aa[1]    posedge
1              aa[1]    negedge
1              aa[2]    posedge
***0***        aa[2]    negedge
***0***        aa[3]    posedge
1              aa[3]    negedge
Summary
Toggle coverage is         : 25%
Number of toggles executed : 1
Number of toggles considered: 4
```

In the above example only bit aa[1] has made a full toggle with a positive edge and negative edge transition, so this is the only bit that is entered into the summary list. Bit aa[0] has no toggle activity whatsoever, while bits aa[2] and aa[3] have made a single excursion as a positive edge and negative edge respectively. All of these bit-signals need further verification effort to be deployed in improving the quality and number of vectors supplied by the test bench. Figure 6-14 shows how toggle coverage would be reported graphically in Verification Navigator.

Figure 6-14

TRIGGERING COVERAGE

Triggering coverage is normally applied to designs written using the VHDL hardware description language. It checks that every signal in the sensitivity list of a PROCESS or a WAIT statement changes without any other signal changing at the same time. The following listings show two practical examples of how triggering coverage can be used to uncover 'logical' design problems.

```
PROCESS (reset1, reset2)
BEGIN
    shut_down_the_system;
END PROCESS;
```

Here the process contains an important action that will be activated whenever either of the two input signals reset1 or reset2 changes state. It could be that an error exists in that the designer did not actually intend to shut down the system via the reset2 signal. If the test bench always results in reset1 changing whenever reset2 changes, then this error would not be detected without a coverage analysis tool. The listing below shows another example of a possible design problem.

```
PROCESS (reset1, reset2)
BEGIN
    IF reset1'EVENT THEN
        b <= reset1;
    ELSIF reset2'EVENT THEN
        c <= reset2;
    END IF;
END PROCESS;
```

Here, because of the order of priority within the `IF...ELSIF` block, the assignment to signal `c` would not occur if signals `reset1` and `reset2` were to change simultaneously. This behavior may not be the intention of the designer and would be highlighted if triggering coverage were used during the testing phase.

Triggering coverage also provides useful information as to the overall synchronous or asynchronous nature of the system by indicating if inputs to processes are changing simultaneously. Figure 6-15 shows how triggering coverage would be reported graphically in Verification Navigator.

Figure 6-15

The above example shows that only 5 out of the 12 signals, in the sensitivity list for the Arbiter, have triggered the process. Signals that have not triggered the process are highlighted so they can be visually isolated easily.

SIGNAL TRACING COVERAGE

Signal tracing coverage has a slightly different terminology and interpretation depending on whether the Verilog or VHDL hardware design language is being used. If Verilog is being used then signal tracing coverage is known as variable trace coverage and checks that variables (i.e. nets and registers) and combinations of variables take a range of values. If on the other hand VHDL is being used as the design language then signal tracing coverage will check that signals and combinations of signals within VHDL architectures take a range of values.

A data file, which is normally formatted as a simple text file, defines the names of the signals/variables to be traced, the type-declaration for the signals/variables and the lowest and highest possible values of the signals/variables to be traced.

Signal tracing coverage can be used in situations where a signal/variable represents the state of a system. For instance where a variable is used to represent the state register of a Finite State Machine (FSM). Whenever a change in any of the selected variables is detected, the current values of all the variables is logged and used to build up a variable trace table. Selecting more than one signal/variable for analysis with tracing coverage allows the state of several FSMs to be monitored, so that the logged values of the signals/variables represent a particular concurrent state of the system. Signal tracing can also be used to monitor any combination of input variables to a block and thus can be extremely useful at the functional or black box testing level.

An example of how signal tracing coverage would be reported by a typical coverage analysis tool in textual format is shown below.

```
Signal trace coverage information

Signal name    Lowest value    Highest value
    Done            0               1
    LSB             0               1

Signal value combinations

   Count         Done      LSB
     3             0         0
     1             1         0
     3             0         1
     0             1         1
```

The tabulated information shows that input combination for Done=1, LSB=1 did not occur as shown by the zero execution count in the first column of the table. The above example used the following signal trace definition file to specify the signals to be traced.

```
Signal_name    Signal_type
   Done            bit
   LSB             bit
```

If the signals had been a vector (i.e. BIT_VECTOR, STD_VECTOR, STD_ULOGIC_VECTOR) rather than a single bit, then the lower and upper bounds (i.e. the tracing range) for each signal would need to be specified in the definition file, e.g:

```
signal_name signal_type lower_value  upper_value
```

DEALING WITH INFORMATION OVERLOAD

Most coverage analysis tools are capable of producing vast quantities of information especially if a designer switches on all the coverage measurements for the whole of the design hierarchy. This means that in some situations the use of coverage analysis tools can be counter-productive as the designer ends up spending more time sifting through vast amounts of information rather than fixing design errors. The user obviously needs to be offered some method of filtering or extracting information for selective parts of the design. In this way the user can be directed to the areas of the design that need the most attention. Some of the methods that can be employed with coverage analysis tools to avoid overloading a user with too much information are:

- Only collect pertinent information.

- View selective parts of the design with a hierarchy browser.

- Filter the coverage analysis results.

- Rank the results in order of seriousness.

- Exclude sections of HDL code.

Although the first method (i.e. only collect pertinent information) appears to be fairly obvious, it is amazing how many times this simple fact is overlooked which means that in a number of situations valuable time is wasted collecting and deciphering unnecessary data. As has been stated earlier, one useful guideline for a verification engineer is to concentrate on achieving 100% statement and branch coverage before using the more powerful coverage measurements. It therefore makes sense to restrict initial data collection to just statement and branch when using a coverage analysis tool.

Most complex projects are normally built up from smaller and usually less complex building blocks. Some of these building blocks may be newly designed and carry a degree of risk as they are unproven, while others may have been taken from an established project where they have undergone extensive testing. Another useful guideline for the verification engineer is to partition the complex design into smaller manageable blocks so that effort can be concentrated on those areas that carry the greatest risk. The majority of coverage analysis tools have a hierarchy browser that enables a verification engineer to rapidly traverse the hierarchy and navigate to the 'problem' areas. Figure 6-16 shows how the hierarchy browser has been implemented in Verification Navigator.

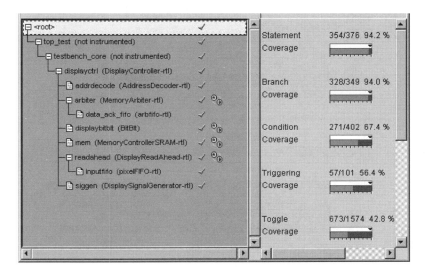

Figure 6-16

In the above example the user is presented with a split window. The left-hand section of the window is the hierarchy browser and gives an overall view of the hierarchy and shows how the various modules or units are related to each other. The right-hand section of the window gives a summary of the various coverage analysis measurements for the part of the hierarchy that has been selected. In this particular case the hierarchy browser is viewing the design from the root of the project, so the information shown in the left-hand part of the window represents a global summary of the results for the whole project. If a module in another part of the hierarchy is selected, by pointing and clicking on the appropriate part of the hierarchy browser, then the information displayed in the right-hand section of the window will change accordingly. The tick marks that appear in the left-hand window are used to visually indicate which parts of the hierarchy browser are being reported in the summary window.

Another useful facility that most coverage analysis tools have is a mechanism to filter the coverage results by temporarily turning off the reporting of one or more of the coverage metrics. This has the effect of reducing the amount of data that is presented to the user and therefore helps to direct the user quickly to the problem areas within the HDL code. Figure 6-17 shows how TransEDA have implemented filtering in their Verification Navigator coverage analysis tool.

Figure 6-17

The above example shows how filtering of the coverage analysis measurements has been applied at the module level (upper figure) using a series of tabs that are selected by the user. The lower figure, in the above example, shows how filtering at the detailed code level is achieved using a series of check-buttons that activate or deactivate the appropriate coverage analysis measurement. In the extreme case, all but statement coverage could be turned off to isolate the basic coding problems associated with the HDL. Then additional check-buttons could be activated to cover the more involved stages of verification. Again the judicial use of color-coding is important as it can make the interpretation of the results easier to assimilate and understand for the user.

Another method of reducing the information overload is to rank the results using some suitable criteria. The ranking could be based on the 'seriousness of the error', with the modules that have the most number of errors being presented first. Alternatively, ranking could be based on simply listing the modules in alphanumeric order. Figure 6-18 shows how ranking has been implemented in Verification Navigator.

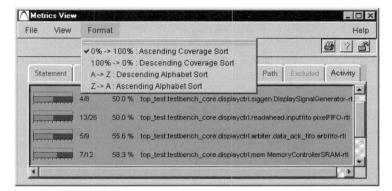

Figure 6-18

The above description gives practical guidelines for dealing with the information overload that can result when coverage analysis is applied to every module and unit in the design project. Another method is to exclude complete or partial sections of HDL code from the analysis and reporting phases of coverage analysis, thereby saving valuable time at the detailed verification stage.

EXCLUDING CODE

As it normal practice to set up a batch file to define the HDL source files that are to be analyzed by the coverage analysis tool, it is a simple matter to delete the file or not include it in the list to prevent it from being analyzed. Some coverage analysis tools allow the user to exclude one or more lines of HDL code in various sections of the source files. This is particular useful in situations where a CASE or nested IF constructs contain a 'default' block that is not normally executed. For example, a block of code that is only executed under error conditions to print out an error message. In this situation is would be extremely difficult to obtain 100% statement covered. By excluding the 'default' block of code, coverage can be improved and the possible target of 100% reached. Obviously it would be unwise for a verification engineer to exclude all the HDL code in a module in order to achieve 100% coverage, so most coverage analysis tools safeguard this situation by reporting on excluded lines of code that have been executed. In practical terms this means that code that should be excluded is usually identified with in-line markers that turn-off and turn-on the coverage analysis locally within the HDL file. An alternative method is to apply post-simulation results filtering to the coverage data. Normally this is achieved graphically by allowing the user to dynamically mark the lines of code that are to be excluded. This process is often know as 'on the fly code exclusion.'

POST-SIMULATION RESULTS FILTERING

If coverage analysis were to be applied to the following piece of HDL code it would be impossible to achieve 100% statement and branch coverage because the 'default' clause cannot be exercised. In this particular example it is impossible to execute the 'default' clause because all the possible combinations that A and B could take have already been covered by the individual case-terms contained within the construct.

```
always @ (A or B)
  begin
    case ({A,B})
      0: C <= 0;
      1: C <= 1;
      2: D <= 0;
      3: D <= 1;
      default: $display ("Catch-all");
    endcase
  end
```

Although it is tempting to question the relevance of the 'default' clause in this particular example, as it appears to be superfluous, it is generally regarded as good coding practice to include a 'default' clause (in a Verilog case construct) or a 'when others' clause (in a VHDL case construct) to help improve the efficiency of the synthesis process. The detailed view of the report file, as shown in Figure 6-19, shows that the branch at line 13 has never been executed.

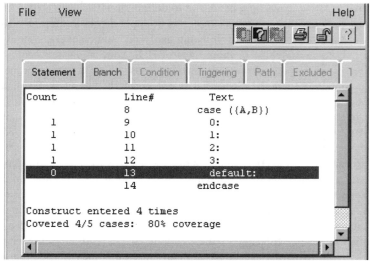

Figure 6-19

As shown in Figure 6-20, selective parts of the HDL code can be marked for filtering by dragging the cursor through the appropriate lines of code (lines 13 and 13a in this example) and then clicking the filter button located at top-right edge of the window.

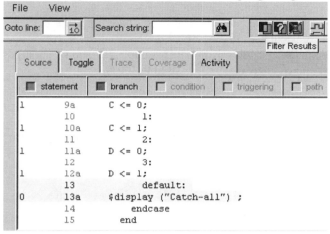

Figure 6-20

This action will cause a mini-window to be displayed where basic information can be recorded for documentation purposes. Figure 6-21 shows how the name of the person responsible for applying the filter and the reason why it was necessary to filter this particular piece of code are recorded. The date/time are automatically inserted.

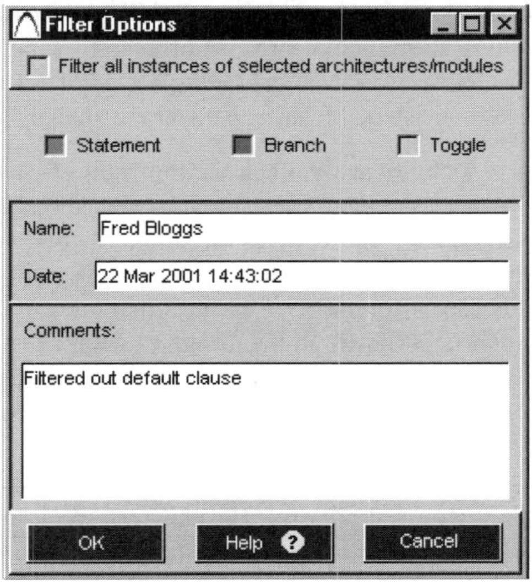

Figure 6-21

One method of showing that one or more lines of code have been filtered-out can be achieved by appending a letter F against the particular module or instance in the window that reports the overall coverage analysis measurements. Figure 6-22 shows how post-simulation results filtering is presented to the user in Verification Navigator. As soon as the 'default' clause is filtered out, the coverage results are automatically recalculated (by Verification Navigator) and the updated results displayed to the user. In this particular example, as shown in Figure 6-22, the statement and branch coverage has increased to 100%.

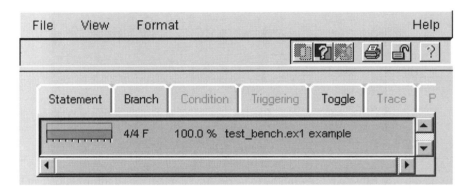

Figure 6-22

Each time a user filters or un-filters a section of HDL a text file is updated in the background which is used to maintain a record of exactly what is currently filtered within each module or instance. As well as holding basic documentation information, the text file also ensures consistency from one coverage analysis run to another.

A set of three buttons, which are available at the top-right of each main window, are used to control the filtering facility. The button on the left filters any highlighted section while the button on the right removes the filter. The button surmounted with a question mark interrogates the text file (maintained by Verification Navigator) and displays the current filtering information. This information can optionally be printed and used for documentation purposes on the design project.

Figure 6-23

Although the above example has shown how a section of HDL code can be filtered, it is also possible to filter out one or more complete modules or instances. For example a designer may be using a block of IP (Intellectual Property) or some legacy code that has been verified previously on another project. Providing the designer is confident that the verification procedures that were applied to these blocks of code were of a sufficiently high standard then any need for further testing can be avoided.

Figure 6-24 shows how module or instance filtering is achieved by selecting the appropriate items in the hierarchy view window and then clicking the filter button on the top-right of the window.

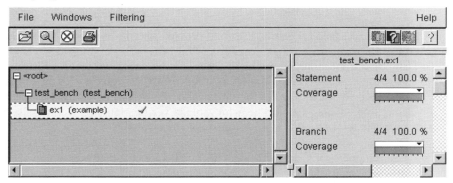

Figure 6-24

Whenever a complete module or instance is filtered-out this fact is shown to the user by greying out the coverage values on the coverage analysis measurements window. An example of how this situation is conveyed to the user is shown in Figure 6-25.

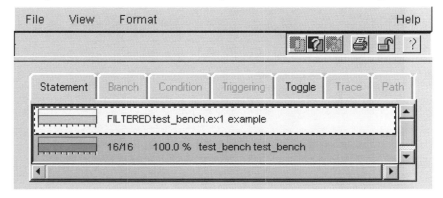

Figure 6-25

SUMMARY

The guidelines that have been introduced in this chapter are summarised below.

- Wherever possible always partition the overall design into sub-modules or sub-units so that the functional boundaries are obvious and well defined.

- Avoid wasting valuable simulation time by collecting only the coverage data that is actually needed. For example, during the initial verification phase, probably only statement and branch information needs to be collected.

- Concentrate the verification effort on proving that the control logic of each module or unit operates correctly. The initial target should be 100% statement and branch coverage. Once this has been achieved additional coverage measurements, such as condition coverage, path and toggle coverage can be applied to the unit or module. Although a target of 100% condition coverage should be achievable, a verification engineer may have to accept a lower value of 85% for path coverage.

- Use statement, branch, condition, path and toggle coverage measurements to prove the control paths in each unit or module.

- Use toggle coverage and variable/signal tracing coverage measurements to prove the data paths and interaction between the various units or modules in the design.

- Make use of the facilities offered by the chosen coverage analysis tool to avoid information overload e.g. hierarchy manager, filtering and code exclusion.

Chapter 7

Coverage
Directed
Verification
Methodology

COVERAGE ANALYSIS IN THE DESIGN FLOW

As discussed in an earlier chapter, coverage analysis can be applied at any (or all) of three stages in the design flow, namely, at the behavioral level of the design, at the RTL level, and at the gate level. Most time is usually spent at the RTL stage. Transforming designs to gate level is almost a fully automatic process and relatively little time, if any at all, is spent doing behavioral design. There are two likely reasons for this lack of time spent at the behavioral level. First, a behavioral description is very far removed from the actual implementation of the design and, second, there is no automatic route to a physical device from behavioral level and, because designers are under pressure to get to the 'real design' they relate to RTL and gates more readily than abstract behavioral descriptions.

COVERAGE ANALYSIS AT BEHAVIORAL LEVEL

Simulation is still carried out at the behavioral level to ensure that the ideas captured comply with the design specification. It is therefore appropriate to use coverage analysis at the behavioral level to ensure that the whole description is verified. The behavioral description is much smaller than the RTL description because it is a higher-level form of the design and as such it is appropriate to run coverage analysis only on the full behavioral description as it nears completion.

Behavioral descriptions contain abstract types such as real numbers and enumerated types and records of types (in VHDL) and the code tends to be written in large procedural blocks (processes, functions, procedures, always blocks, and tasks). It is for this reason that not all coverage analysis measurements are appropriate at behavioral level.

Toggle coverage is concerned with simple binary signals which are less common in behavioral descriptions therefore in general toggle coverage is not appropriate.

The measurements that test procedural code such as statement, branch, condition and expression, path and triggering coverage should be used on the behavioral design.

COVERAGE ANALYSIS AT RTL

We have already seen that the RTL design process is very complex and results in large descriptions and that the process has to be subdivided to make it more manageable and to allow a larger design team to work on the project. To recap Figure 7-1 shows the three parts of the RTL design process - module design, subsystem integration and system integration.

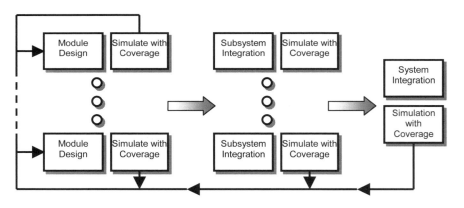

Figure 7-1

At the module design stage the descriptions are relatively simple and the simulations tend to be short. It is appropriate to ensure that the module is thoroughly verified before it is integrated into the subsystem, as problems are harder to track down as the design complexity increases. Coverage analysis should be employed as part of this thorough module verification. In order to ensure that a module has been completely verified all coverage measurements should be used at this stage.

At the subsystem integration stage the simulations are becoming longer, up to a few hours each, and the subsystems are likely to consist of large amounts of RTL code. The amount of data that can be produced by a coverage analysis tool can be extremely large and the overhead on the simulations - although only a small percentage - can be significant in actual time. It is still essential to ensure that module interfaces and 'glue logic' is thoroughly verified and that each module's behavior is fully tested within the subsystem. It is for this reason that it is sensible to use a subset of the coverage measurements. As an absolute minimum it is essential to check that every statement has been executed and every branch decision has been taken. In addition toggle coverage ensures that a minimum range of data values has been passed through the design. Finally it is important to verify every expression has been thoroughly tested. Subsystem integration is not a trivial process therefore coverage analysis should be used throughout the subsystem design phase in order to ensure that any integration problems are trapped early and not left to cause problems at a later stage. This is shown graphically in Figure 7-2.

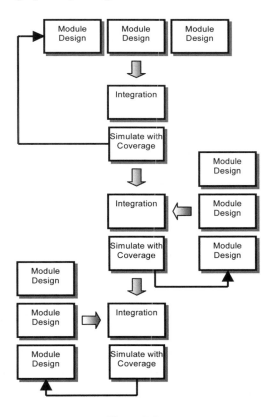

Figure 7-2

System integration is very similar to subsystem integration except that the blocks being integrated are significantly larger - as are the quantity and duration of the simulations at this stage. It is therefore appropriate to only use a subset of coverage measurements at the system integration level. We would recommend the same measurements used at subsystem level, that is - statement, branch, condition and toggle coverage. Time pressure, however may dictate that less coverage information is collected to make simulations shorter and to reduce the time required to analyze the coverage results. If this is the case the absolute minimum measurements we would recommend are statement and branch coverage.

Figure 7-3 summarises the coverage measurements that should be used at each stage of the RTL design process.

	Statement	Branch	Condition	Toggle	Path	Triggering
Module Design	✓	✓	✓	✓	✓	✓
Sub-System Integration	✓	✓	✓	✓		
System Integration	✓	✓	✓ ☆	✓ ☆		

☆ - Recommended

Figure 7-3

COVERAGE ANALYSIS AND TRANSIENT BEHAVIOR

HDL simulations can contain transient behavior because of the order in which assignments are executed during the simulation. The temporary signal value changes caused by this transient behavior are often referred to as glitches. These glitches result in lines of code being executed but the results of the execution are overwritten in the same time step.

Figures 7-4 and 7-5 show examples of Verilog code and VHDL code respectively which will create glitches on signal `d` when the signals `a` and `b` both change simultaneously.

```
always @ (a)

    c <= !a;

always @ (b or c)

    d = !d;
```

Figure 7-4

```
PROCESS (a)

    BEGIN

        c <= not a;

END PROCESS;


PROCESS (b, c)

    BEGIN

        d <= not d;

END PROCESS;
```

Figure 7-5

The examples in figures 7-4 and 7-5 are fairly contrived but it does prove it is very easy to write HDL code that contains glitches.

Glitches in the simulation affect the coverage analysis results, the simulator executes statements because of the glitches and coverage analysis records this execution. The recorded behavior is transient and therefore is not checked by the test bench. This does not make the coverage wrong but it does mean that the transient behavior is not properly tested. It is therefore more useful if the coverage tool can exclude transient behavior from its results. Not all coverage tools have this capability; Verification Navigator from TransEDA is one that does.

COVERAGE ANALYSIS AT GATE LEVEL

At gate level there are no statements and expressions to verify with coverage analysis. The only measurement which is appropriate at gate level, and is available in most coverage tools, is toggle coverage.

One of the other tasks performed during gate level design is fault simulation. The purpose of fault simulation is to create a set of tests to verify the physical device once it has been manufactured. Fault simulation takes a great deal longer than normal simulation; therefore anything that can be done to minimize the time spent doing this will help reduce the overall time spent in gate level design.

Fault detection relies on two characteristics. The first is controllability - ensuring both logical 1 and 0 can be applied to every node in the circuit by applying values to the input pins. The second is observability - ensuring that the effect of a fault on every node can be propagated through the circuit and observed on the output pins. Without a high degree of controllability the fault simulation results will be very poor. By making sure the controllability of the circuit is high before starting fault simulation means that expensive fault simulation time is not wasted.

Toggle coverage is directly proportional to circuit controllability, therefore running a normal simulation with toggle coverage allows you to ensure you have adequate controllability before starting fault simulation.

COVERAGE ANALYSIS AND STATE MACHINES

State machines can be described in RTL code explicitly or implicitly. Explicit descriptions have the state transitions explicitly written as assignments in the HDL code. In implicit state machines the next state logic is written as a series of expressions. It is very difficult to determine state machine behavior by looking at the HDL code of an implicit description. Figures 7-6 and 7-7 show an example of the next state logic for a two-bit counter described explicitly and Figures 7-8 and 7-9 show the implicit form of the same logic.

```
case (state)
    2'b00 :
        next_state = 2'b01;
    2'b01 :
        next_state = 2'b10;
    2'b10 :
        next_state = 2'b11;
    2'b11 :
        next_state = 2'b00;
endcase
```

Figure 7-6

```
CASE state IS
    WHEN "00" =>
        next_state <= "01";
    WHEN "01" =>
        next_state <= "10";
    WHEN "10" =>
        next_state <= "11";
    WHEN "11" =>
        next_state <= "00";
END CASE;
```

Figure 7-7

```
next_state[0] = !state[0];
next_state[1] = (!state[1] && state[0]) || (state[1] && !state[0]);
```

Figure 7-8

```
next_state(0) = NOT state(0);
next_state(1) = (NOT state(1) AND state(0)) OR (state(1)
                AND NOT state(0));
```

Figure 7-9

In terms of verifying state machine coverage, transition coverage on explicit styles will be measured by statement coverage. With implicit styles it is difficult to relate missing coverage to the transitions of the state machines, however 100% condition coverage will ensure that all the behavior is tested.

With state machines it is critical to use a deglitching facility if it exists otherwise transitions that are not actually latched in the state register could be counted because of the transient behavior.

Coverage analysis tools record transition behavior but they do not record the order in which the transitions are executed or sequence of operations of the state machine. To verify sequences have been covered a specific state machine analysis tool such as Verification Navigator's FSM coverage tool from TransEDA is required.

PRACTICAL GUIDE LINES FOR COVERAGE ANALYSIS

All coverage analysis tools can produce a vast amount of information and there is always an overhead associated with collecting this information, therefore you need some practical guidelines for using these tools. We have already discussed the measurements that should be used at different stages in the design process and Figure 7-10 summarizes this information.

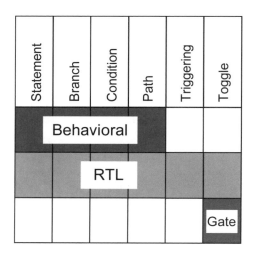

Figure 7-10

By restricting the measurements that you use as the design becomes more complex will help to make the data produced more manageable. The way in which the data is presented is also important. Verification Navigator from TransEDA is particularly good at presenting the information in an easy to understand graphical interface.

We have also discussed glitches in the design behavior and how these can affect the coverage results. Most coverage tools have a deglitching capability. However the overhead of using this is greater than normal and it is therefore recommended that deglitching be used only at the end of each stage in the design process.

In some cases when the coverage tool shows that there is a construct which has not been completely covered due to some constraint in the design it may be impossible to achieve 100% coverage analysis. It is for this reason that the coverage analysis tool should be used as a 'verification advisor'. The tool should be used to measure how much of the design has been verified. Then a design review should be held to determine 1) if it is possible to achieve a higher coverage with further tests, 2) if the uncovered part of the design has functionality which is no longer required, and therefore can be removed from the design and 3) if the omitted coverage is acceptable within the scope of the design. This process is shown in Figure 7-11.

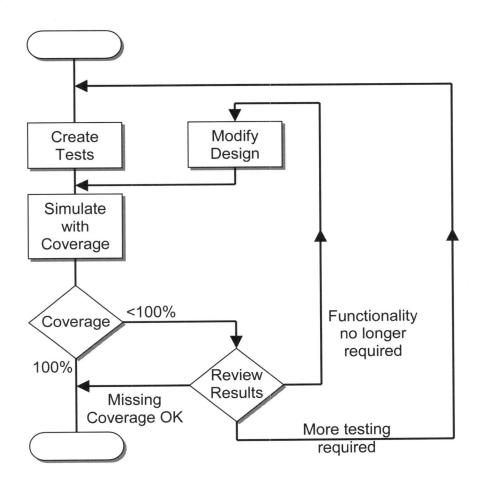

Figure 7-11

COVERAGE ANALYSIS AS A VERIFICATION ADVISOR

Software tools are produced to help people with their design and verification tasks. That is why we feel that you should not be a slave to the coverage figures and should not necessarily strive for 100% coverage if it does not make sense within the scope of your design. It is however up to you as design and verification engineers to decide what parts of the missing coverage are important to you. Figure 7-12 shows the sort of coverage analysis targets that should be aimed for.

COVERAGE MEASUREMENTS AND TARGETS

Measurement	Coverage Test (%)
Statement	100
Branch	100
Condition	60 – 100*
Path	>50
Triggering	100
Toggle	100

* Depending on Coverage tool

Figure 7-12

Every statement and branch of your code should be executed. The only exceptions to this rule are error checking code - which should not normally be executed - and extra case or if branches which are added for synthesis tools. Some coverage analysis tools allow meta comments to exclude such code from consideration to make the review process simpler.

It should be possible to toggle every signal in your design, the only exceptions should be constant signals such as power and ground.

In terms of testing expressions, the value that should be aimed for is dependent on which coverage analysis tool you are using. Not all 2^N combinations (where N is the number of inputs) are generally required to fully verify an expression. In most cases it is $2N + 1$. This makes a significant difference to the verification time. For example a 4 input expression can have 16 possible input combinations but usually only 5 of these are required to fully verify the expression. Some coverage analysis tools take account of this fact. For example Verification Navigator has a measurement called Focused Expression Coverage. When using such tools, a high percentage condition coverage should be aimed for. If your coverage analysis tool mandates that you must test your expressions with all possible input combinations then it is unlikely that you will be able to achieve a high percentage and a figure of 60% may be the best that can be achieved.

Not all coverage tools contain path coverage and the value you should aim for is very much dependent on your design style. If your paths are independent - that is signals in the first branching construct of a path are not reassigned or used in the second - then path coverage is not important. Figure 7-13 shows such an example.

```
if (ctl1)
    base = 0;
else
    base = 2;
if (div_sel)
    result = acc / denom;
else
    result = acc;
```

Figure 7-13

Figure 7-14 shows an example of paths that are not independent and therefore path coverage is important. In this example a divide-by-zero error could be missed if the paths are not fully verified. We have already suggested that path coverage should be used at module level verification therefore it should be relatively simple to review the path coverage results and determine if the missing coverage is significant.

```
if (ctl1)
    base = 0;
else
    base = 2;
if (div_sel)
    result = acc / base;
else
    result = acc;
```

Figure 7-14

A high percentage process triggering coverage should also be obtained otherwise the process sensitivity list may in fact be wrong and could lead to different behavior after synthesis.

SAVING SIMULATION TIME

The final key to using your coverage tool effectively is to minimize the simulation overhead by only turning coverage on for the parts of the design that you are interested in. This may be because you are running full chip simulation but are only interested in verifying a small part of the total design, or you have already achieved a desirable level of coverage on the rest of the design and you are adding tests to increase the coverage on a particular part. In either case there is no need to record coverage information you are not going to use.

NUMBER OF COVERAGE ANALYSIS LICENSES REQUIRED

As discussed earlier, coverage analysis should be performed at the module level. This means that every engineer performing verification at this stage must have access to the coverage analysis tool. As a general approximation one coverage license between three engineers should be sufficient because the simulation runs are fairly short at this stage. The ideal would be a one-to-one correspondence between verification engineers and coverage licenses.

The major problem is running coverage on subsystem and system regression tests, in general at this stage in the design process the verification team runs many simulations in parallel. If you have a limited number of coverage licenses, the number of coverage simulations which can be run in parallel is limited, and therefore the time to run the regression tests is extended significantly. An example of this is shown in Figure 7-15. The ideal solution is to have the same number of coverage simulation licenses as simulator licenses. If this is not possible because of project budgets, a workable minimum ratio is between 3:1 to 5:1 simulator to coverage licenses.

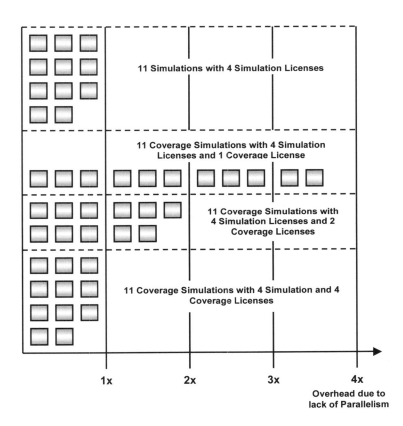

Figure 7-15

This page is intentionally left blank.

Chapter 8

*Finite
State
Machine
Coverage*

FSM COVERAGE

Finite state machine (FSM) coverage deserves special attention given the important role FSMs play in describing the control functionality in many designs. It has been shown in several technical papers and publications how developing tests to increase FSM coverage has detected difficult-to-find bugs. Traditional coverage analysis tools have provided the following FSM metrics:

- Visited state coverage, ensures that every state of an FSM has been visited.

- Arc coverage, ensures that each arc between FSM states has been traversed.

Design teams often aim for over 95% coverage on these metrics, but it is possible to achieve even 100% state and arc coverage without exercising all the functionality of the FSM. Thus visited state and arc coverage do not necessarily measure the extent to which the functionality of the FSM has been verified. As a result coverage analysis tools have introduced a metrics referred to as FSM sequences or paths to measure a path through a sequence of visited states or arcs.

FSM PATH COVERAGE

With this new metric comes the difficult task of describing and measuring an FSM path. Consider a simple FSM such as the one shown in Figure 8-1 below.

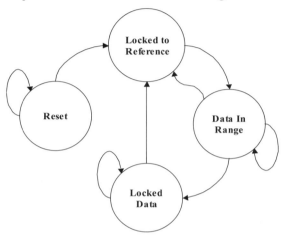

Figure 8-1

Looking at the FSM you can see that it has the following functionality:

- Wait in *Reset* until locked to a reference.

- Acquire data.

- If the reference is lost go to *Locked to Reference*.

A series of arcs that traverses every arc in the FSM at least once is known as an arc tour. Completing an arc tour of the FSM would involve the following path of state and arcs through the FSM:

1. Reset-->Reset
2. Reset-->Locked_to_Reference
3. Locked_to_Reference-->Data_In_Range-->Locked_to_Reference
4. Locked_to_Reference-->Data_In_Range-->Locked_Data-->Locked_to_Reference

These are the basic paths through the FSM and embody the main functionality of the FSM. There are two arcs missing that are needed to complete the tour; they are the same-state loop in the states *Data_In_Range* and *Locked_to_Data*.

REACHABILITY BASED PATH EXTRACTION

Some coverage analysis tools automatically perform a reachability analysis of the FSM's states. From this analysis they then derive what are known as sequences which are the paths between each state and every other reachable state. Apart from the *Reset*, in our simple example, every state is reachable from every other state and these tools would generate the following nine different paths.

1. Reset-->Locked_to_Reference
2. Reset-->Locked_to_Reference-->Data_In_Range
3. Reset-->Locked_to_Reference-->Data_In_Range-->Locked_Data
4. Locked_to_Reference-->Data_In_Range
5. Locked_to_Reference-->Data_In_Range-->Locked_Data
6. Data_In_Range-->Locked_Data
7. Data_In_Range-->Locked_to_Reference
8. Locked_Data-->Locked_to_Reference
9. Locked_Data--> Locked_to_Reference-->Data_In_Range

For this simple FSM there are already nine paths and this analysis has not accounted for the same-state loops on *Data_In_Range* and *Locked_Data*.

The reachability analysis does not account for these same-state loops in generating the paths. However, if the analysis does not account for same-state loops the FSM's ability to wait will not have been verified. Since the reachability analysis does not know how many times the same-state loop may have been taken it cannot account for these loops as part of its analysis. So while this automatic method saves you the preparation time it misses the critical same-state loops and increases your analysis effort and time as you filter out the redundant paths and generate paths for the additional important functionality.

MANUAL PATH SPECIFICATION

Other coverage analysis tools do not provide any automatic methods of path extraction, but they do provide you with a manual way to specify the path using a series of states and some wildcards (*=0+, ?=1+). This increases your preparation time as you identify and specify these paths, however it saves you analysis time. For the above FSM you would need to manually specify the following:

1. Reset-->Reset?
2. Reset?-->Locked_to_Reference
3. Locked_to_Reference-->Data_In_Range?--> Locked_to_Reference
4. (Locked_to_Reference-->Data_In_Range?)?-->Locked_Data?-->Locked_to_reference
5. Locked_to_Reference-->Data_In_Range-->Data_In_Range?
6. Locked_to_Reference-->Data_In_Range-->Locked_Data-->Locked_Data?

When you have manually specified the paths with wildcards there are fewer paths than were generated automatically by the reachability analysis, but you needed to study the FSM and then manually describe the paths to the coverage tool.

TRANSEDA'S FSM PATH APPROACH

The FSM path coverage metric in TransEDA's VN-Cover Coverage Analysis solution automatically provides a compact, meaningful set of FSM paths enabling deeper insight into a design during verification. TransEDA's unique approach avoids the overwhelming quantity of paths generated by simple reachability analysis and reduces the time required to specify paths manually. VN-Cover's FSM path metric automatically provides a complete representation of a FSM's functionality while minimizing the complexity. This results in shorter analysis time and improved verification productivity. VN-Cover automatically extracts all FSM paths and provides a concise metric that fully represents the FSM paths. Critical in this ability to concisely represent FSM paths and their coverage is to:

- Separate the FSM's initialization behavior from cyclic behavior.

- Identify cyclic behavior in the FSM.

- Combine small cycles into the larger cycles that may be present in a FSM.

- Allow measurement of paths reached compared with possible paths.

The result of this analysis is that it allows you to focus on the FSM's functionality.

FOCUS ON FUNCTIONALITY

By identifying the cyclic behavior, VN-Cover's FSM path metric provides a representation of the design's functionality without you being lost in the details. Three types of paths are then used to describe FSM's functionality:

- *A link* is a directed set of states that does not repeat.
  An example would be an initialization sequence.

- *A cycle* is a directed set of states that returns to its starting state without passing through any state more than once.

- *A supercycle* is a longer cycle that identifies the high level functionality and provides a concise summary of the overall structure of the FSM.

Supercycles and cycles allow patterns representing important functionality in the FSM to be automatically recognized. Supercycles report design functionality that is not always apparent to the user when looking at the FSM. Using VN-Cover on the simple FSM example, as shown in Figure 8-1, it would report that there are three supercycles.

Supercycle 1

The first supercycle would be the *Reset* state's same-state loop as shown below.

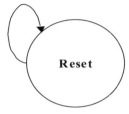

Figure 8-2

This represents the functionality of the FSM to wait in *Reset* until it has *Locked to Reference*. Once it has then this state is linked to the FSM's main functionality.

Supercycle 2

The second supercycle, shown below, represents the FSM's main functionality.

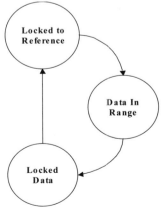

Figure 8-3

This is the FSM's correct operational functionality. It describes that the FSM must first be *Locked to Reference*, then get *Data In Range*, and finally *Locked Data.*

Supercycle 3

The third supercycle, shown below, is the FSM's secondary functionality.

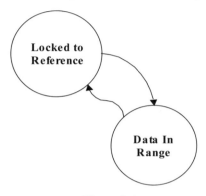

Figure 8-4

This represents the functionality when an error occurs and the reference is lost. The system has to abandon data acquisition and start over again. This automatic extraction of functionality into supercycles, cycles, and links shortens the analysis time and makes it easier for the designer and verification engineer to develop additional vectors for the unverified functionality resulting in shorter verification effort.

SIMPLIFY COMPLEXITY

Hanging off these supercycles would be several smaller cycles. These cycles represent a wide range of things. They can be temporal characteristics, corner cases, or border conditions of a supercycle's functionality. For supercycle 2, shown in Figure 8-3, there would be two cycles. The first cycle, as shown in Figure 8-5, would be the same-state loop that would occur while the FSM was in state *Data In Range* waiting for the data to come into range.

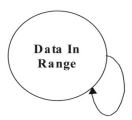

Figure 8-5

The second cycle, as shown below, would be the same-state loop that would occur while the FSM was in state *Locked Data* waiting for the data to be locked into the system.

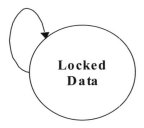

Figure 8-6

For supercycle 3 shown in Figure 8-4 there would be one cycle. The cycle is in common with Supercycle 2 and is the same-state loop that would occur while the FSM was in state *Data In Range* waiting for the data to be in range. Functionally, this cycle could be covered by either supercycle as in both cases the path to this cycle is the same: Locking the reference and waiting more than one clock period in the *Data In Range* state. This shows that the three supercycles:

- Reset

- Locked_to_Reference-->Data_In_Range-->Locked_Data

- Locked_to_Reference-->Data_In_Range

and the following two cycles:

- Data_In_Range

- Locked_Data

describe the functionality of the FSM. The only thing that is missing now is the link from *Reset* to the main functionality of the FSM as shown below.

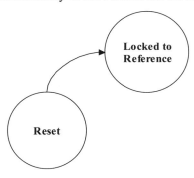

Figure 8-7

Including this link will provide you with the complete representation of the state machine:

- Reset-->Locked_to_Reference

This new FSM path coverage metric, supported by the concept of links, cycles and supercycles, is a valuable new measure of verification completeness necessary for Coverage Closure.

A COMPLEX EXAMPLE

Many people consider the JTAG TAP Controller to be a relatively simple FSM. However, if you look at Figure 8-8 and considered enumerating all of the paths of states and arcs through it you would quickly decide that maybe it is not so simple after all.

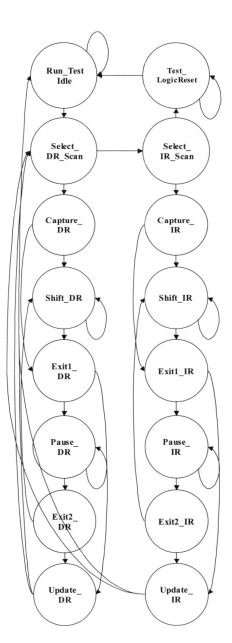

Figure 8-8

Using VN-Cover's FSM Path analysis on the FSM shown in Figure 8-8, detects two simple supercycles that represent the overall functionality of the TAP controller:

1. Test_Logic_Reset same-state loop
2. Test_Logic_Reset-->Run_TestlIdle-->Select_DR_Scan-->Select_IR_Scan

The first supercycle is the *Run_Test1Idle* same-state loop and it represents the important functionality of the FSM to wait in the idle state.

The second supercycle, as shown in Figure 8-9, represents the overall functionality of the FSM, which is to select and scan the Data Register and or select and scan the Instruction Register.

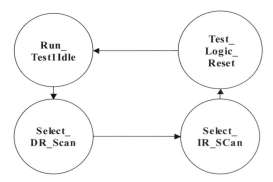

Figure 8-9

VN-Cover's path analysis also detected the smaller cycles that are the paths through the data and instructions registers:

- Cycles through the Data Register that start and end at Run_TestIdle.

- Cycles through the Instruction Register that start and end at Run_TestIdle.

- Cycles through the Data Register that start and end at Select_DR_Scan.

- Cycles through the Instruction Register that start and end at Select_DR_Scan.

There were also some smaller same-state loops and two smaller loops one each in the instruction and data register. The full set of cycles are listed in Figure 8-10 at the end of this chapter.

VN-Cover's FSM path analysis resulted in the following:

- Two Supercycle representing the FSM's main functionality.

- 23 Cycles representing the functionality of the smaller cycles in the FSM.

- There are no Links in this particular FSM.

Taken together these FSM paths clearly describe the functionality of the FSM in easy to understand pieces. This higher level of abstraction provides you with improved verification productivity and shorter analysis time because you can easily understand what is the unverified functionality. If you had used the reachability analysis available from other coverage analysis tools where there would have been a total of 240 FSM paths. Most of these 240 paths would be redundant sequences, but it still would not have included the behavior represented by the same-state loops. You can also contrast this with having to analyze the FSM and then manually write your own sequences.

If you did this you would find that the best that you can create by hand are 25 paths that are almost identical to the ones automatically generated by VN-Cover. You can see a listing of those paths in Figures 8-10 to 8-14 at the end of this chapter.

CONCLUSION

This chapter has described the importance of FSM path coverage and how TransEDA's FSM path coverage metric provides an automatic and efficient way to see, understand and verify the functionality represented by FSMs. This unique coverage metric provides users with more useful information than is traditionally found in coverage analysis tools, enabling designs to be released sooner and with more confidence.

Appendix-E provides a set of worked examples that show how VN-Cover is used to analyze state, arc and path coverage for a finite state machine.

The following figures and listing show the full set of cycles for the Tap controller as mentioned in the first part of this chapter.

CYCLES AUTOMATICALLY EXTRACTED BY VN-COVER

Listed below are the cycles that were automatically extracted by VN-Cover.

---

1. Run_TestIdle-->Select_DR_Scan-->Capture_DR-->Shift_DR-->Exit1_DR-->Pause_DR-->Exit2_DR-->Update_DR

2. Run_TestIdle-->Select_DR_Scan-->Capture_DR-->Shift_DR-->Exit1_DR-->Update_DR

3. Run_TestIdle-->Select_DR_Scan-->Capture_DR-->Exit1_DR-->Pause_DR-->Exit2_DR-->Update_DR

4. Run_TestIdle-->Select_DR_Scan-->Capture_DR-->Exit1_DR-->Update_DR

5. Run_TestIdle-->Select_DR_Scan-->Select_IR_Scan-->Capture_IR-->Shift_IR-->Exit1_IR-->Pause_IR-->Exit2_IR-->Update_IR

6. Run_TestIdle-->Select_DR_Scan-->Select_IR_Scan-->Capture_IR-->Shift_IR-->Exit1_IR-->Update_IR

7. Run_TestIdle-->Select_DR_Scan-->Select_IR_Scan-->Capture_IR-->Exit1_IR-->Pause_IR-->Exit2_IR-->Update_IR

8. Run_TestIdle-->Select_DR_Scan-->Select_IR_Scan-->Capture_IR-->Exit1_IR-->Update_IR

9. Select_DR_Scan-->Capture_DR-->Shift_DR-->Exit1_DR-->Pause_DR-->Exit2_DR-->Update_DR

10. Select_DR_Scan-->Capture_DR-->Shift_DR-->Exit1_DR-->Update_DR

11. Select_DR_Scan-->Capture_DR-->Exit1_DR-->Pause_DR-->Exit2_DR-->Update_DR

12. Select_DR_Scan-->Capture_DR-->Exit1_DR-->Update_DR

13. Select_DR_Scan-->Select_IR_Scan-->Capture_IR-->Shift_IR-->Exit1_IR-->Pause_IR-->Exit2_IR-->Update_IR

14. Select_DR_Scan-->Select_IR_Scan-->Capture_IR-->Shift_IR-->Exit1_IR-->Update_IR

15. Select_DR_Scan-->Select_IR_Scan-->Capture_IR-->Exit1_IR-->Pause_IR-->Exit2_IR-->Update_IR

16. Select_DR_Scan-->Select_IR_Scan-->Capture_IR-->Exit1_IR-->Update_IR

17. Run_TestIdle

18. Pause_DR

19. Shift_DR

20. Pause_IR

21. Shift_IR

22. Exit1_DR-->Pause_DR-->Exit2_DR-->Shift_DR

23. Exit1_IR-->Pause_IR-->Exit2_IR-->Shift_IR

Figure 8-10

Figure 8-11 below shows cycles 1 through 4 for the TAP controller.

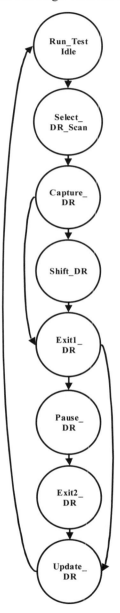

Figure 8-11

If you inspect cycles 5 through 8, in Figure 8-10, you will see that there is a similar set of cycles that to relate to the instruction register rather than the data register.

Figure 8-12 below shows cycles 9 through 12 for the TAP controller.

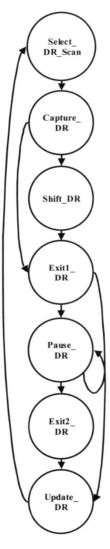

Figure 8-12

Again, if you inspect cycles 13 through 16, in Figure 8-10, you will see that there is a similar set of cycles as in Figure 8-12 above that relate to the instruction register rather than the data register.

There are also some same-state loops with each of the Supercycles that enable the state machine to wait. Lastly there are two cycles for the backward loop contained in both the data and instruction register.

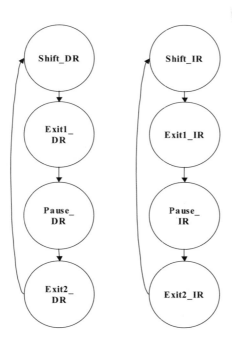

Figure 8-13

MANUALLY CREATED PATHS FOR TAP CONTROLLER

If you analyzed the TAP controller manually and then wrote a set of paths to fully represent its functionality the best that you can create by hand are 25 paths. You will notice that the paths shown in Figure 8-14 below are almost identical to the ones automatically generated by VN-Cover in Figure 8-10.

1. Test_Logic_Reset-->Test_Logic_Reset?

2. Test_Logic_Reset-->Run_TestIIdle?-->Select_DR_Scan-->Select_IR_Scan

3. Run_Test1Idle-->Select_DR_Scan-->Capture_DR-->Shift_DR?-->Exit1_DR-->Pause_DR?-->Exit2_DR-->Update_DR-->Run_Test1Idle

4. Run_Test1Idle-->Select_DR_Scan-->Capture_DR-->Shift_DR?-->Exit1_DR-->Update_DR-->Run_Test1Idle

5. Run_Test1Idle-->Select_DR_Scan-->Capture_DR-->Exit1_DR-->Pause_DR?-->Exit2_DR-->Update_DR-->Run_Test1Idle

6. Run_Test1Idle-->Select_DR_Scan-->Capture_DR-->Exit1_DR--> Update_DR-->Run_Test1Idle

7. Run_TestIdle-->Select_DR_Scan-->Select_IR_Scan-->Capture_IR-->Shift_IR?-->Exit1_IR-->Pause_IR?-->Exit2_IR-->Update_IR--

>Run_Test1Idle

8. Run_TestIdle-->Select_DR_Scan-->Select_IR_Scan-->Capture_IR-->Shift_IR?-->Exit1_IR-->Update_IR-->Run_Test1Idle

9. Run_TestIdle-->Select_DR_Scan-->Select_IR_Scan-->Capture_IR-->Exit1_IR-->Pause_IR?-->Exit2_IR-->Update_IR-->Run_Test1Idle

10. Run_TestIdle-->Select_DR_Scan-->Select_IR_Scan-->Capture_IR-->Exit1_IR-->Update_IR-->Run_Test1Idle

11. Select_DR_Scan-->Capture_DR-->Shift_DR?-->Exit1_DR-->Pause_DR?-->Exit2_DR-->Update_DR-->Select_DR_Scan

12. Select_DR_Scan-->Capture_DR-->Shift_DR?-->Exit1_DR-->Update_DR-->Select_DR_Scan

13. Select_DR_Scan-->Capture_DR-->Exit1_DR-->Pause_DR?-->Exit2_DR-->Update_DR-->Select_DR_Scan

14. Select_DR_Scan-->Capture_DR-->Exit1_DR-->Update_DR-->Select_DR_Scan

15. Select_DR_Scan-->Select_IR_Scan-->Capture_IR-->Shift_IR?-->Exit1_IR-->Pause_IR?-->Exit2_IR-->Update_IR-->Select_DR_Scan

16. Select_DR_Scan-->Select_IR_Scan-->Capture_IR-->Shift_IR?-->Exit1_IR-->Update_IR-->Select_DR_Scan

17. Select_DR_Scan-->Select_IR_Scan-->Capture_IR-->Exit1_IR-->Pause_IR?-->Exit2_IR-->Update_IR-->Select_DR_Scan

18. Select_DR_Scan-->Select_IR_Scan-->Capture_IR-->Exit1_IR-->Update_IR-->Select_DR_Scan

19. Run_TestIdle.Run_TestIdle?

20. Pause_DR.Pause_DR?

21. Shift_DR.Shift_DR?

22. Pause_IR.Pause_IR?

23. Shift_IR.Shift_IR?

24. Exit1_DR-->Pause_DR?-->Exit2_DR-->Shift_DR?

25. Exit1_IR-->Pause_IR?-->Exit2_IR-->Shift_IR?

Figure 8-14

Chapter 9

Dynamic
Property
Checking

STRUCTURAL TESTING

The verification techniques that have been described so far in this manual have focused on checking how much of the HDL code has been covered or exercised. This involved, in the case of Verilog or VHDL, applying various measurements to check the amount of statement, branch, condition, path and toggle coverage. An additional set of measurements, namely FSM state, FSM arc and FSM path as described in Chapter 8, can be used to verify designs containing finite state machines. These measurements collectively perform what is called structural testing or white box/ open box testing. One of the primary objectives of structural testing, as mentioned in Chapter 6, is to raise the designer's confidence level that the HDL code does not contain any untested areas.

Although measuring how much of the HDL code has been covered is important, it does not verify that a design operates in a functionally correct manner. For example, consider the situation, in Figure 9-1, where a group of functionally related signals need to be checked to make sure their behavior matches the design's specification.

Some of the things a designer might want to check are:

- Was DEVSEL deasserted on the next clock pulse after FRAME' went *high*?

- Did TRDY go *low* before a maximum of 16 clocks had occurred?

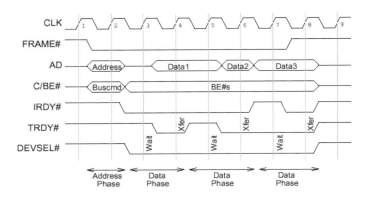

Figure 9-1

So how does a designer check whether the results obtained from the simulation match the original specification for the design?

VISUAL CHECKING

Probably the oldest and most labour intensive technique is based on visually checking the simulation results against the formal specification. Clearly the success of this technique relies very much on the determination and dedication of the individual who is doing the checking. Also each time a change is made to the HDL code the same amount of effort needs to be deployed to check the simulation results all over again.

SELF-CHECKING TEST BENCHES

Another technique is to write a self-checking test bench that checks the actual results obtained from the simulation against the expected results. Although this technique can dramatically reduce the amount of effort needed to re-check a design after a change has been made to the HDL code, it does require considerably more effort during the initial test bench creation phase. For example, the designer needs to spend time working out what the results should be after certain test vectors have been applied to the design and then write a series of comparison tests. This can consume quite a lot of effort, as during the early phases when the self-checking test bench is being developed a designer may not be sure whether the test bench is inadequate (i.e. fails the comparison test for some reason) or the HDL model is not working correctly.

PATTERN MATCHING

This technique relies on the ability to perform the following two tasks

1. Describe the original specification of the HDL design in some sort of language that can be handled by a computer.

2. Collect the simulation results in a compact and machine readable format.

Once the above information has been gathered a computer program can be used to automatically check and compare the above details. The pattern matching technique is attractive because once the design's specification has been captured the amount of effort needed to re-check the operation of the circuit after a change has been made is minimal.

Properties

The first thing to consider is how the design's specification can be described or captured. One of the most common method uses what are called properties that specifies the value on signal(s) at point(s) in time in relation to other signal(s). For example, a property could define that the state of signal 'x' should be checked on each rising-edge of the main clock to see when it becomes a logic '1'. Once signal 'x' becomes true the next property is then considered and checked. This property might define that signal 'x' can remain in the logic '1' state for a maximum of up to 4 clocks before going to the logic '0' state. Once a set of properties have been written they can be grouped together to form the specification for a model.

Although at the time of producing this manual there is no recognized standard for writing properties, the Accellera Formal Verification Technical Committee has been created to develop and promote a property specification language compatible with both the Verilog (IEEE-1364) and VHDL (IEEE-1076) hardware description language standards. Further information regarding developments in this area can be found on Accellera's web site: *www.accellera.org*

The next part of this manual explores how the concept of using properties to check the behaviour of a circuit can be combined with code and FSM coverage to augment the coverage directed verification methodology that was described in Chapter 7.

VERIFICATION FLOW

Up until this point the various coverage metrics that have been described in this manual have been treated as a series of separate tools each of which checks a certain aspect of the design. The technique of using properties to describe the behavior within a design can be used to tie the various coverage measurements together and thus form an effective and productive testing strategy. Figure 9-2 shows a flowchart of a testing strategy based on a coverage directed verification process using properties.

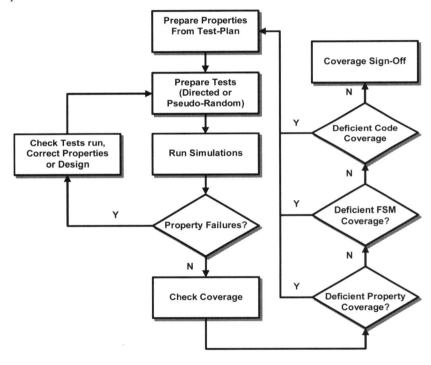

Figure 9-2

The strategy starts at the test planning stage where the various properties are identified that will be needed in order to show that the design behaves according to its original specification. These properties fall into two distinct sets called 'expected behavior' and 'prohibited behavior'. An example of a property describing an expected behavior is, "If A happens and B and C happens then D will happen." If this behavior is observed during the simulation then the property is reported as covered. It should be noted that dynamic property checking cannot formally prove these properties to be true: this will always be the case without exhaustive simulation.

However, dynamic property checking does provide a measurable degree of confidence in their correctness.

An example of a property describing a prohibited behavior is, "A will never happen." If "A" happens during simulation, then the property is violated and proven false. A set of tests (which could be a directed set of tests or pseudo random tests) are prepared to check that all the properties have been exercised correctly during the simulation. Any failures that are detected at this stage could be attributed to an inaccuracy in the description of a property or an inadequacy in the design. This may mean re-checking the test plan to make sure the original property definitions have been correctly specified or carrying out further diagnostic work on how the design was implemented. In general property failures at this stage can be attributed to prohibited behavior that is not wanted occurring during the simulation.

The coverage checking phase is entered once there are no further property failures. This consists of three phases namely: dynamic property coverage, followed by FSM coverage and finally code coverage. Deficient property coverage at this stage can be traced to an expected behavior not being detected during the simulation of the design. To rectify this situation additional test vectors will be needed to ensure that the expected behavior occurs at least once during the simulation of the design.

When all property failures have been eradicated and all expected behaviors have been covered, the next thing to check is FSM coverage. The first thing to do is make sure that all the states and arcs of the key FSMs have been covered and then check that the main FSM paths have been exercised. Deficiencies in FSM coverage indicates gaps in the test plan, which should be filled by preparing more properties and tests. Once FSM coverage has reached an acceptable level the code coverage metrics should be checked. Again, any code coverage deficiencies indicate that the test plan should be revisited and more tests and properties prepared.

Coverage sign-off can take place once the user-specified sign-off criteria for each of the above three major coverage measuring methods has been achieved.

DYNAMIC PROPERTY CHECKING IN OPERATION

Dynamic property checking can be divided into the following three distinct phases.

1. Analyze the details (i.e. signal names) that occur within the property definitions. This information is used to compile a list of the signals that need to be traced during the simulation.

2. Run a simulation during which time a tabular trace file is generated.

3. Compare the contents of the tabular trace file with the property definitions.

Collecting Simulation Results

Most Verilog and VHDL simulators have the capability of outputting the simulation results as a tabular trace file as well as or instead of a waveform diagram. Although the physical size of the file used to hold a waveform diagram can become excessively large, a tabular trace file is much smaller in comparison as the information is held in a very compact format.

As an example, consider the waveform diagram for the two signals shown in the figure below.

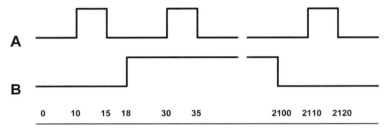

Figure 9-3

The activity for the two signals can be expressed in a very compact tabular format, as shown by Figure 9-4, by listing the times when either signal 'A' or 'B' makes a change. At time zero both signals are at logic '0'. Initially there is some activity with signal 'A' making a couple of full transitions at time-units 10 and 30, and signal 'B' going high at time-unit 18. This is followed by a long gap until at time-unit 2100 signal 'B' goes low. Finally both signals return to a low state at time-unit 2120.

Time	A	B
0	0	0
10	1	0
15	0	0
18	0	1
30	1	1
35	0	1
2100	0	0
2110	1	0
2120	0	0

Figure 9-4

Figure 9-5 shows the preparatory stage that is used to extract the names of the signals from the property definition files and build a list of the signals to be traced during the logic simulation.

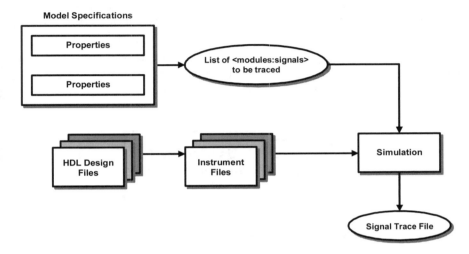

Figure 9-5

Once the simulation has run to completion the signal trace file will contain a detailed record of the activity within the circuit. All that remains is to compare the information in the signal trace file with the definitions in the property files. Basically this is a pattern matching exercise as shown by Figure 9-6.

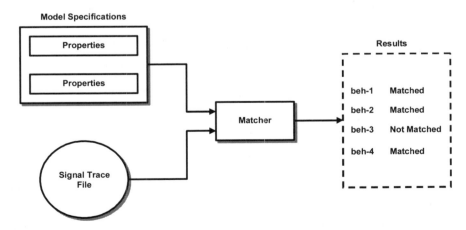

Figure 9-6

Typical method of implementation

VN-Property DX from TransEDA is a tool that offers dynamic property checking. The way this particular tool has implemented dynamic property checking is by taking advantage of the powerful pattern matching facilities inherent in the Perl scripting language. This is then coupled to the tabular tracing capability as described above.

Consider the Device Under Test (DUT) as shown in Figure 9-7 and the situation where a set of properties need to be created to check the functional relationship of the signals in the DUT with respect to the main clock (i.e. clk).

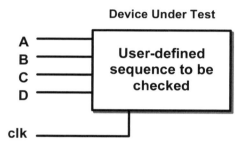

Figure 9-7

The figure below shows the ways in which a Perl regular expression can be used to perform various pattern matching tests.

"Greedy" Quantifier	"Lazy" Quantifier	Allowed Range
{n, m}	{n,m}?	At least *n* times, no more than *m* times
{n, }	{n, }?	At least *n* times
{n}	{n}?	Must occur exactly *n* times
*	*?	0 or more times (same as {0,})
+	+?	1 or more times (same as {1,})
?	??	0 or 1 time (same as {0, 1})

Figure 9-8

The 'Greedy' quantifier looks for as many matches as possible, while the 'Lazy' quantifier looks for the minimum number of matches (which could be just one).

Let us assume that the particular behavior that is being searched for starts with signal 'A' being true for 3 clock cycles before signal 'B' becomes true.

The behavior continues with the option that signal 'C' may become true before signal 'D' occurs, which marks the end of the complete behavior. This behavior can be expressed, using the Perl regular expression quantifiers, as: A{3}BC*D.

If on consecutive clock pulses, the input signals to the DUT exhibited this pattern:
BAAABDDAAAABCCDA

then the following two sequences would be matched.

AAABD and AAABCCD

The listing, as shown in Figure 9-9, shows how a series of properties could be used within VN-Property DX to define and check the sequence: A{3}BC*D.

```
package RegExpExampleSeq;
use vars qw(@ISA);
@ISA=qw(Sequence);
sub begin
{
  my $self = shift;
  return
    {
      'clock' => '$dut:clk',
      'clocking_edge' => 'rising',
      'steps' =>
        [
          {
            'test' => sub {$dut:A = = 1 },
            'quantifier' => 3
          },
          {
            'test' => sub {$dut:B = = 1 },
            'quantifier' => 1
          },
          {
            'test' => sub {$dut:C = = 1 },
            'quantifier' => '*'
          },
          {
            'test' => sub {$dut:D = = 1 },
            'quantifier' => 1
          }
        ]
    };
}
1; #End of the package file (must return 1)
```

Figure 9-9

Although it is outside the scope of this manual to go into detail about the Perl scripting langauge, the following notes may prove useful in understanding the listing shown in Figure 9-9.

Notes:

1. A Perl package is used to encapsulate the properties used by VN-Property DX.

2. The module: use vars qw(@ISA); predeclares all variables whose names are in the list, allowing use of them under use strict and disabling typo warnings.

3. The Perl package inherits the contents of the tabular trace file (i.e. simulation results) using the special array called @ISA.

4. $self = shift; sets up an anonymous reference to the Perl hash which is used as the main object for any functions called within the Perl package.

5. The scalar signal (i.e. the clock) which is used as the reference point for all the tests is defined with: 'clock' => '$dut:clk';
    Where "dut" is the name of the HDL module and "clk" is the name of the signal within the module that will be used as the reference.

6. The active edge of the clock is defined with: 'clock_edge' => 'rising | falling'

7. Each one of the tests, that are contained in the main body of the Perl package, applies a check for a particular property. For example, the first test checks that signal 'A' has been true (i.e. logic '1') for 3 consecutive clocks before moving on to perform the next test. If any one of the tests should fail, then the checking procedure returns to the very first test and waits for that test to be satisfied before moving onto the next test.

8. A default value of '1' will be used if the quantifier value is omitted. This means that the second and fourth tests in Figure 9-9 could have been reduced to:

    { 'test' => sub {$dut:B == 1 }, }

    { 'test' => sub {$dut:D == 1 }, }

Appendix F shows how VN-Property DX is used to collect and check dynamic properties in a typical HDL design.

Appendix G gives some examples of how properties can be developed to describe the behavior of a set of functionally related signals within a finite state machine.

Chapter 10

Verification Architecture for Pre-Silicon Validation

INTRODUCTION

The dramatic increase in the number of gates that are available in modern integrated circuits coupled with the use of IP cores and advances in design re-use methodologies are contributing to larger, more complex and highly integrated designs. This increase in complexity results in designs that take increasingly more effort and time to verify. As explained in earlier chapters, verification tasks commonly accounts for 50% to 80% of the chip's development schedule.

RTL (Register Transfer Level) coding in Verilog and/or VHDL is the implementation methodology of choice for most chips. RTL simulation is the most common verification methodology for these chips. This chapter outlines how dynamic simulation based pre-silicon validation can be performed with a well thought out, proven verification architecture.

First of all, let us first consider the following facts:

It takes an inordinate amount of time to build the test benches (a.k.a. "test jig") to test every level of integration starting at the module level. Even if the modules are thoroughly tested in their own right, integration verification is mandatory and is a daunting task. A chip may have standard bus or interconnect interfaces and interface verification is a difficult task. A chip may have to work with other components in the system and unexpected system component interaction can result in system failure.

As a result we observe that, in real practice, most chip development groups perform some module-level verification, preferring to spend their time in full-chip or system-level verification. While 70% of the chip development time is spent in verification, 65% of that verification time is spent in the following three activities:

- Setting up the simulation environment (10%)

- Functional HDL verification (15%)

- System verification (40%)

When we analyze where the verification time is spent we notice that verification has three major components:

- Test creation

- Test execution

- Results checking.

Test creation and results checking take up the majority of time spent on verification. Test execution time varies greatly depending on the type of design, the simulator or hardware emulator used. In the case of hardware emulators there is an overhead in compiling and maintaining the hardware that needs to be traded off with the raw performance achieved in simulated clocks over software simulators.

Raw performance in terms of the numbers of clocks per second simulated does not necessarily translate well into a high-quality verification environment. Designers need to focus on quality instead of quantity of simulation. This means that a designer needs to consider how high-quality tests can be manually or automatically created and what trade-offs can be made.

The key objective of the verification effort is to ensure that the fabricated chip works in the real environment. Quite often development groups wait until prototypes are built in order to find out if this objective was met in a phase called "prototype validation". The cost of not having met this objective can be very severe.

This chapter outlines a strategy for pre-silicon validation that has been used by many blue-chip development groups to successfully deliver first-pass shippable silicon.

While first-pass shippable silicon also requires that circuit, timing, package and such other aspects of implementation are correct as well, we also need to consider functional verification and validation. Functional verification is one of the primary tasks that normally consumes the major amount of time and effort for the development project group.

PRE-SILICON VALIDATION

Pre-silicon validation is generally performed at a chip, multi-chip or system level. The objective of pre-silicon validation is to verify the correctness and sufficiency of the design. This approach typically requires modelling the complete system, where the model of the design under test may be RTL, and other components of the system may be behavioral or bus functional models. The goal is to subject the DUT (design under test) to real-world-like input stimuli.

The characteristics of pre-silicon validation are as follows:

- It validates design correctness.

- It may be used for implementation or intent verification.

- It does not rely on a design specification or golden reference model.

- It uncovers unexpected system component interactions, inadequate or missing functionality in RTL.

- Manually specifying expected results or output at a low level is difficult.

Outlined below are the major considerations for a pre-silicon validation strategy.

Concurrency

Most complex chips have multiple ports or interfaces and there is concurrent, asynchronous and independent activity at these ports in a real system. A system-level verification environment should be able to create and handle such real-world concurrency to qualify as a pre-silicon validation environment. Concurrency needs to be handled in both the test controller and the bus/interface models used.

Some models will return data when a transaction completes, so the test controller or environment can do data checking. Other models require the expected data to be provided up front so the model can do data checking when the transaction completes. Such behavior impacts the test checking methodology and the amount of concurrency that can be generated.

Results Checking

While it may be relatively easy to generate activity or stimulate the different ports or interfaces of a chip, the difficult part is to implement an automated results or data checking strategy. In a system-level pre-silicon validation environment, designers are relieved of maintaining or keeping track of the data in test code, simplifying the task considerably for a multi-ported system.

Automated Test Generation

One must first consider the test creation and/or generation methodology. The test generation methodology is closely interrelated to the results checking strategy. For example, *will you dynamically check the results while the test is running, or will you post-process the results?* The answer to this question quite often depends on the type of application where the chip is being used.

Utilizing the generate/run/post-process method in a design with concurrency requires extensive intelligence of the checker or a very detailed reference model that resolves all of the ordering and predicts the final state of the system.

A dynamic test generator and checker are more effective in creating very interesting, reactive test sequences. They are more efficient because errors can be detected as they happen. In a generate/run/post-process method, one may run a simulation for eight hours, only to find during the post-process checking that an error occurred 20 minutes into the simulation, with the balance of the simulation time being useless.

In directed testing, users specify the sequence of events to generate. This is efficient for verifying known cases and conditions. Pseudo-random testing is useful in uncovering unknown conditions or corner cases.

Pseudo-random test generation, where transactions are generated from user-defined constraints, can be interspersed with blocks of directed sequences of transactions at periodic intervals to re-create real-life traffic scenarios in a pre-silicon validation environment.

Dynamic test generation also facilitates reactive test generation. Reactive test generation implies a change in test generation when a monitored event is detected during simulation.

Robust, High-quality Verification IP

The quality of verification, and therefore the probability of shippable first-pass silicon, is greatly enhanced with robust, high-quality verification IP, which includes such items as BFMs (bus functional models) and protocol monitors.

A common mistake is to require the project group that develops the RTL to also create the verification IP used to verify the RTL. While this is sometimes required for proprietary interfaces, it runs the risk of making the same wrong assumptions.

Further, the rate of maturity of an internally developed model is much slower than a commercial model that has been used by multiple independent design groups, provided the supplier is responsive and diligent in increasing the model quality from its customer feedback.

Whether the design team builds or buys the verification IP, they must ensure that the models can fit into the test generation and checking strategy that is adopted. Also, the models need to operate in a mode that fits into a pseudo-random test methodology. Models that load and execute a pre-compiled test sequence do not work in an environment where a designer dynamically generates and check tests.

Models must operate at the appropriate level of abstraction, concurrency and programmable controllability:

- Some processor BFMs simply drive transactions on the bus, but do not automatically handle deferred transactions and retries. They have no concept of cache coherency. The test generator, or some layer of intelligence added by the user, has to handle all of the bus-specific details that could affect the order of transaction completion, and thus, the final "correct" data values.

- Some models can generate multiple transactions concurrently; some perform only one transaction at a time. Models that generate multiple transactions simultaneously may complete these transactions in an arbitrary order depending on bus timing and other concurrent traffic. If the completion order is non-deterministic, then the test generator will have to gain visibility into the system to determine the final state.

- Some models represent "real" devices, and always generate or respond to signals on the bus with the same timing. To fully validate adherence to a bus protocol, the system must be tested with all possible variations in cycle timing that is allowed by the device specification. This means that the test generator should be able to change the timing of the models, and to randomly vary delays and cycle relationships, such as data wait states and snoop stalls.

Ease of Use

With the considerable pressure that is already applied to shortening the timescales that are used on most projects, design teams need to focus on completing designs and delivering shippable chips. It therefore does not make much sense to send design engineers to a training class in order to learn a new language or methodology to implement a verification strategy. A better alternative is to have a verification environment that is easy to use and intuitive as this will have a dramatic effect in increasing a designer's productivity level.

Leveraging Design and Application Knowledge

A general system-level verification environment may generate many impertinent scenarios or false errors. It is necessary that the verification tool or environment be capable of leveraging application-specific knowledge so that only the pertinent application space is tested.

Right Level of Abstraction

When a problem is difficult to solve, changing the level of abstraction at which the problem is viewed often is the key to solving it. The complexity of today's chips makes it impossible or extremely arduous to deal with bit-level signals in an interface. It is necessary to operate at the transaction level or higher level of abstraction.

Debugging

The manifestation of a problem occurs further down in simulation time from the root cause, because of the time it takes to propagate the flaw to an observable point. Ideally, but not always practical, it is best to catch a problem closer to the root cause. So, a verification environment should facilitate analysis and make it easy to trace back to the root cause of the problem.

Configurability

A system-level pre-silicon validation environment should be easily configurable, since multiple different configurations will need to be tested for a thorough system-level verification.

Reusing the Test Environment

A well-thought-out verification strategy will consider re-use of tests and the verification environment for successive revisions and generations of chips. Since test creation is one of the most time-consuming and labour-intensive parts of the verification process, designers should consider leveraging on subsequent projects the verification environment and the test suites already developed.

Machine Cycles Become Less Expensive

Many companies are using server farms to operate a verification environment that runs for 24 hrs a day 7 days a week. Linux-based server farms appear to be cost effective and easy to manage. Load balancing requirements can be easily solved with commercial tools.

Quite often, the progress in a chip development project is fix-rate limited early in the design, and as the design stabilizes, progress becomes find-rate limited. The server farm operating on a 24 x 7 basis is most useful in the find-rate limited phase of the project.

In lieu of server farms, some companies use hardware-accelerated simulation where the RTL and some portion of the test bench is mapped into gates inside an emulator or hardware accelerator. Ideally, the maximum speed-up in simulation performance will be achieved if the entire RTL and test bench is mapped into hardware. However, a completely synthesizable test bench is not always practical or effective.

When considering hardware-accelerated simulation, it is important to consider what parts of the test bench will be in hardware, what parts will be in a software simulation environment, and how the two will communicate. It is also possible to map transactors, or bus functional models, into hardware while keeping the test controller in a software simulation environment.

Whether utilizing a server farm or hardware accelerated simulation, it is important to consider upfront how the test execution machine will be kept supplied with different and interesting stimuli to simulate. An automated test generation environment or tool is imperative.

AN ARCHITECTURE FOR PRE-SILICON VALIDATION

To perform pre-silicon validation, a designer needs to consider the verification architecture and the verification components necessary. To facilitate reuse and extensibility, the verification environment should be flexible enough to utilize different models for a plug-and-play, modular architecture.

Figure 10-1 shows a pre-silicon validation architecture that has been successfully used by major companies over a number of years.

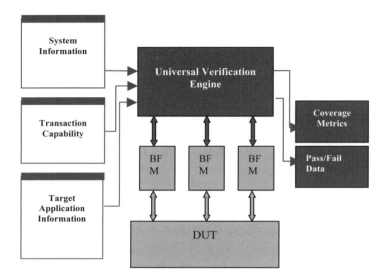

Figure 10-1

Verification components

The major components for this verification approach are:

- Intelligent bus functional models of processors and i/o interfaces

- Intelligent bus protocol monitors

- Intelligent test controller and data checker

Intelligent Bus Functional Models

An intelligent BFM provides a transaction-level API, and is designed to handle concurrency and parallelism. This makes it suitable to be used in an automated test generation environment. It provides a consistent programmer's view. It also offers a high degree of controllability for the model behavior to emulate a real device with real operating characteristics through programmable delay registers and configuration registers.

Intelligent Bus Protocol Monitors

An intelligent bus protocol monitor provides dynamic protocol checking and can be used in automated test generation environments. It provides dynamic bus state information, which can be used to provide dynamic feedback to user tests or automated test controllers. It should also be extensible to accommodate user-defined sequences.

Intelligent Test Controller and Data Checker

An intelligent test controller utilizes BFMs and transaction generators to create constraint-based concurrent sequences of transactions at the different interfaces of the design under verification. An intelligent test controller can generate transactions pseudo-randomly, for a user specified sequence, or a mix of both. It can also perform specific tasks or dynamically reload input constraints upon a certain event occurring during simulation. In addition to test stimuli generation, an intelligent controller also provides for automated and dynamic data checking.

CONCLUSION

System-level verification requires a well thought out, proven strategy to achieve shippable first-pass silicon. This chapter has outlined the key features to consider about a system-level verification environment and the key components of a verification architecture to achieve pre-silicon validation with the ultimate goal being shippable first-pass silicon.

This page is intentionally left blank.

Chapter 11

Overview of Test Bench Requirements

The descriptions that have been presented so far in this manual have assumed that the coverage tool is used to analyze a single results file that has been produced by a single test bench. This sounds like a very neat, tidy and very controlled environment. In reality things are very different with maybe hundreds or thousands of test benches being used to exercise different parts of the total design. This means that a verification engineer is faced with managing a huge volume of data.

This chapter therefore concentrates on explaining how a verification engineer can identify the most productive and useful test benches that should be included in the various test suites.

BASIC TEST BENCH CONSTRUCTION

In its most basic form a test bench is simply a mechanism that generates a certain stimulus and applies this to a design or DUT (device under test). The response, produced by the device under test, is subsequently checked or measured against some pre-defined criteria and a decision made as to whether that particular test was successful or not. So basically a test bench contains a stimulus generator, which is connected to the device under test, and a response analyzer that could take various forms as will be described later in this chapter. Figure 11-1 shows a typical test bench incorporating a device under test, stimulus generator and results analyzer.

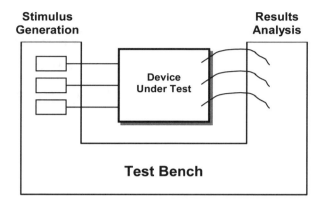

Stimulus Generation   **Results Analysis**

Device Under Test

Test Bench

Figure 11-1

The stimulus generator is responsible for generating the correct sequence and phasing of the input waveforms for the device under test. This may take the form of producing a simple waveform that has a repetitive pattern or makes changes at well defined times. Free running clocks and data signals can be created using behavioral coding techniques in the Verilog or VHDL languages. Alternatively a detailed list, which could be a process block or an external data file, describing when each change takes place can be constructed and used to drive the device under test. This simple technique can be repeated, by using multiple process blocks, to generate a set of synchronised waveforms. For example, a free running clock signal, a reset signal and some data and control signals that operate in a synchronous fashion.

Complex signals that may have variations in their edge-to-edge timing relationships involve considerably more effort on the part of the verification engineer in order to achieve accurate modelling. Quite often the solution here is to include some form of random element that is used to modify the strict timing of the waveforms and hence introduce a certain degree of uncertainty with the rising/falling edges of the signals.

The other part of the problem is checking whether the results obtained when the design is simulated with the appropriate test bench are correct or not (i.e. results analysis). Although there are various ways for the results to be analyzed, probably the three most common methods are: visual inspection of the responses, visual inspection of the waveforms or using a self-checking test bench. The first two methods are very labour intensive as they involve inspecting either ASCII printouts or studying graphical information to identify when certain signals made specific changes and whether these changes happened at the correct point in the simulation. These methods are also error prone as they rely on the skills and experience of the verification engineer to detect obscure problems and understand complex interactions between signals. The third method is much more formal and is based on analyzing the behavior of the design before simulation and predicting what state a signal should be in at a certain time. The test bench is then built to check that what was predicted matches what actually happened. Although this method potentially gives the verification engineer a high degree of confidence in the quality of the final design it does involve a considerable amount of effort in developing a realistic self-checking test bench. A better and more productive solution is to use a coverage analysis tool to help 'tune' the test bench to achieve maximum coverage of the device under test.

COVERAGE DIRECTED TEST BENCHES

Figure 11-2 illustrates how a coverage analysis tool can be used to complement the verification engineer's testing strategy by showing the parts of the device under test where there is inadequate coverage. The verification engineer can then make adjustments to the stimulus generator in the test bench, or modifications to the HDL code in the appropriate module or sub-unit to improve the amount of coverage.

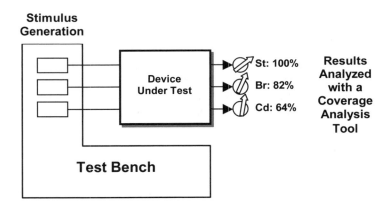

Figure 11-2

TEST BENCH FOR A SINGLE MODULE OR SINGLE UNIT

Throughout this manual it has been stressed that working at the single module or single unit level is beneficial as:

• The size of the design is smaller and simulation time is shorter.

• The functionality of the design is normally easier to understand.

• The number of inputs/outputs is normally less and therefore more manageable.

• The boundaries are better defined and accessible.

The strategy of partitioning the overall design into smaller modules or units and spending time validating each block can be highly productive because, once a block has been fully validated, it can be used as a system component with little or no further detailed verification effort. For example the coverage measurements described in Chapter 6 could be used to validate a unit at the white box or open box level to prove that the control paths are correct. When the unit is used at the sub-system level and combined with other units, that have also been fully validated, they can all be treated as black boxes which means that the verification engineer can concentrate on just checking the data paths and functional boundaries between the units.

Designing a test bench for a small single unit should be fairly straightforward as the number and complexity of the signals that have to be generated is generally limited. As the unit forms just one part of the sub-system, its functionality should also be easy to comprehend and model in the test bench. This means that for a simple unit it should theoretically be possible to develop a single comprehensive test bench.

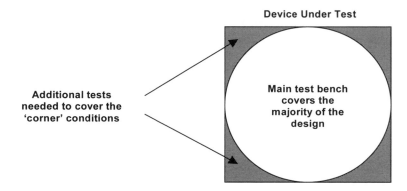

Figure 11-3

In reality it is probably found that when the coverage results are examined the initial comprehensive test bench does not actually cover the whole unit and extra tests need to be developed, as illustrated in Figure 11-3, to achieve full coverage. These extra tests may be incorporated into the original 'comprehensive' test bench or may be developed as stand alone test benches to satisfy the 'corner' tests. In either case the amount of effort is not unreasonable and one person or a small verification team can easily manage the final number of tests.

If the same strategy is applied to sub-system or system testing then the amount of productive work that can be achieved drops as it becomes impossible or too time consuming to create one comprehensive test bench. What normally happens is a whole series or large suites of test benches are developed by one or more people to exercise particular sections of the overall design.

DEALING WITH MULTIPLE TEST BENCHES

It was mentioned earlier in this chapter, that in reality the verification team might develop hundreds or even thousands of test benches during the testing phase of a typical project. This will occur at the module, sub-system and system level.

Figure 11-4 shows how various test benches have been used to check different parts of the overall design.

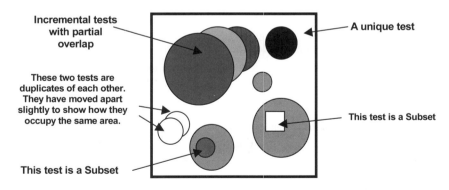

Figure 11-4

As can be seen in Figure 11-4 some of the tests check unique parts of the design while other tests simply extend how much of a particular area of the design have been covered. These are known as unique or incremental tests. Some tests check areas of the design that have already been checked by previous tests and are known as sub-sets or possible redundant tests. There are occasions when one test maps over an area that has been tested in exactly the same way as a previous test. This is known as a duplicate test and again could possibly be redundant. Projects that have large verification teams need to have effective inter-person communication channels and project management techniques in place in order to avoid creating multiple sub-sets or duplicate tests. It is sometimes impossible to avoid creating tests that map over the same part of the design. This is because quite often the logic needs to be placed into a certain state before an action can take place (e.g. a finite state machine needs to be at particular state before data can be clocked into a certain register). So two different tests may need to cycle the logic initially through exactly the same sequence in order to check out two different divergent actions that happen later in time.

IMPROVING YOUR TESTING STRATEGY

As mentioned earlier in this chapter there are a number of techniques that can be used to construct an effective test bench. For example: writing a set of unique test vectors that cause the DUT to cycle through a set of known states; generating an exhaustive set of test vectors that check all the input combinations; injecting error conditions on the inputs and checking that they are detected. Other methods include writing self-checking test benches, and applying (pseudo) random patterns to the inputs. Whichever method is used the final question that needs to be answered is: *"How effective was the test bench?"*

The next chapter describes how to determine the effectiveness of each test bench and how to manage and optimize a test suite that contains a large number of test benches.

Although the in-depth design of test benches is outside the scope of this manual, the reader may find the following publication useful in this respect.

Writing Test Benches - Functional Verification of HDL Models

Author: Janick Bergeron

Published by Kluwer Academic Publishers

ISBN 0-7923-7766-4

Chapter 12

Analyzing and Optimizing the Test Suite

THE TEST SUITE

One of the main objectives faced by the verification engineering team is to try and establish a test suite that contains the minimum set of productive test benches and as few duplicated or repeated tests as possible. If this can be achieved then it will save valuable simulation time whenever an engineering change is made to one or more of the HDL coded modules, by ensuring that only the productive test benches are re-run. The temptation here is that due to the amount of manual effort involved in sorting out which test benches are the best ones to re-run, a verification engineer re-runs the whole suite and reluctantly accepts the ensuing time penalty.

Using a test suite analysis tool, this otherwise labour intensive task can be automated thereby saving considerable time during the verification phase of the project. Probably one of the best-known test suite analysis tools in use today is CoverPlus from TransEDA. Recently this point solution tool has been renamed as VN-Optimize™ and incorporated into the verification environment known as Verification Navigator to form a highly integrated and comprehensive coverage analysis product. The remainder of this chapter uses a number of screen shots to illustrate how this particular test suite analysis tool can be successfully incorporated into the verification phase of the project's design flow.

The set of results, as detailed below, show the percentage of coverage analysis and simulation time that was obtained when the 6 test benches were run independently of each other on part of a design.

Test Bench	%coverage	Simulation Time
test_monitor	71.07	0:00:40
test_monitor1	80.99	0:01:12
test_monitor2	71.07	0:01:15
test_monitor3	71.07	0:01:15
test_monitor4	73.28	0:01:14
test_monitor5	75.48	0:01:13

Table 12-1

Although it is fairly easy to see, from Table 12-1, that test_monitor gave the maximum amount of coverage in the shortest amount of simulation time, it is not immediately obvious how much overlap there is between the other tests and whether any tests possibly duplicate one other.

Figure 12-1 shows the situation immediately after the 6 test bench results files have been read into Verification Navigator. At this stage the history files (i.e. test bench results files) are displayed in random order.

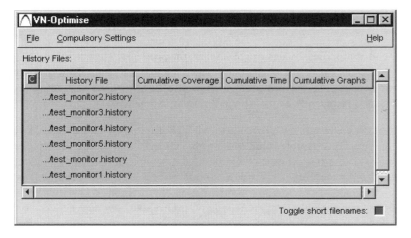

Figure 12-1

The test suite analysis tool within Verification Navigator offers a Sort facility whereby the test bench results are sorted according to a criterion set by the user. An example showing the effect of sorting the results based on statement and branch is shown by Figure 12-2.

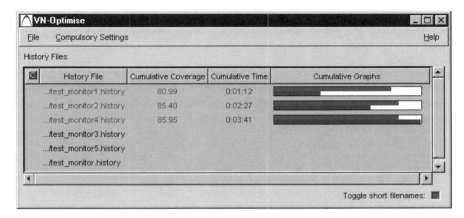

Figure 12-2

As shown in Figure 12-2 `test_monitor1`, `test_monitor2` and `test_monitor4` are the only productive tests for this particular design and that maximum coverage of 85.95% is reached after 3 minutes and 41 seconds of simulation time. The test suite analysis tool achieves this by ranking the results files so that the files that give the maximum amount of coverage in the minimum amount of time are placed in priority order at the top of the list. What is even more revealing is that the other 3 tests (i.e. `test_monitor3`, `test_monitor5` and `test_monitor`) did not increase the amount of coverage; they only wasted valuable simulation time.

Using the information given in Table 12-1 it can be calculated that even with this simple design the last 3 tests actually wasted 3 mins 8 seconds of simulation time. (i.e. `test_monitor3` wasted 1 minute 15 seconds, `test_monitor5` wasted 1 minute 13 seconds, and `test_monitor` wasted 40 seconds.) This wasted time equates to 45.96% of the total simulation time and that dispensing with these tests would save a significant amount of simulation effort.

REGRESSION TESTING

During the development and verification phases of a project, changes can occur that affect the operation of an individual module or unit and potentially how that unit interacts with the remainder of the system. Whenever an ECO (Engineering Change Order) occurs the appropriate suite of tests must be re-run to prove that any changes have not adversely affected the operation of the rest of the system. The verification team is faced with a difficult choice at this stage. Do they re-run all the tests or a unique sub-set? The decision here is between the amount of simulation time that can be devoted to this task and the minimum level of coverage analysis that is deemed acceptable. Most companies tend to approach this problem by establishing a set of sorting criteria based on running the regression test suite on a daily, weekly or monthly basis.

Verification Navigator contains a control panel where a user can set the regression settings that match the needs within their particular company. Figure 12-3 shows the Sorting Criteria panel settings that are typically used for daily regression testing.

Sorting Criteria		
statement	◯ Off	◉ On
branch	◯ Off	◉ On
excluded	◉ Off	◯ On
path	◉ Off	◯ On
condition	◉ Off	◯ On
trigger	◉ Off	◯ On
trace	◉ Off	◯ On
toggle	◉ Off	◯ On

Figure 12-3

Although settings tend to vary from company-to-company, typical settings for weekly coverage are normally based on achieving maximum statement, branch, condition and toggle coverage. Monthly regression settings are normally based on achieving maximum coverage on all coverage settings. An example of how different coverage settings can affect the overall results is shown in Figure 12-4 where a monthly regression setting (i.e. all coverage settings switched-on) has been used.

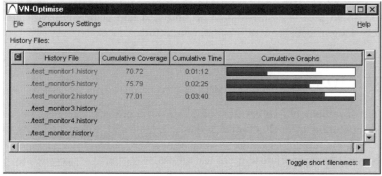

Figure 12-4

Figure 12-4 shows that when the monthly regression settings are used the optimizer tool alters the sequence for running the tests in order to achieve a maximum coverage of 77.01%. In this particular example, the optimized list now includes test_monitor5 between test_monitor1 and test_monitor2. Also test_monitor4 is no longer included in the list as its coverage has already been covered by one or more of the other tests. It should also be noted that the maximum coverage achieved is significantly lower than the coverage that was obtained when the daily sorting criteria was used as in Figure 12-2.

MERGING TEST BENCH RESULTS

Although the examples that have been considered so far in this chapter only contain a small number of results files, it is sometimes convenient to merge one or more test bench results files to speed-up the loading process and improve the readability and interpretation of the messages produced by the test suite analysis tools.

As an example, consider the test bench results files shown in Figure 12-4. The first 2 files could be merged together by selecting the corresponding files and then clicking the Merge button. This action, which is shown in Figure 12-5, creates a new combined file, which in this particular case has a default file name of merged.history. If required, the user can provide an alternative file name to match the naming convention that is used by the verification engineering team.

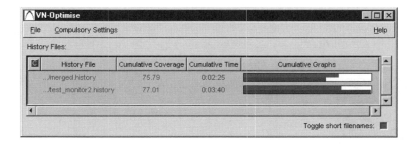

Figure 12-5

OPTIMIZING THE TEST BENCHES

Looking at the results shown in Figure 12-5, it can be seen that the merged results file merged.history gives 75.79% coverage for the design after 2 mins 25 secs of simulation time. The amount of coverage can be increased by 1.22% to 77.01% by including `test_monitor2` in the test suite but this is at the expense of additional simulation time. In this particular case the extra simulation time that is needed to achieve this is 1 min 15 secs. If these figures are expressed as percentages of the original coverage value and simulation time, then they equate to an increase of 1.6% coverage for an increase in 51.7% simulation time. The immediate reaction to these figures prompts the question as to whether `test_monitor2` should be included in the test suite. A better alternative might be to optimize the `merged` test bench file so that it includes the incremental difference that `test_monitor2` contributes. The success of this strategy obviously relies on how much effort it will take to isolate the incremental difference for this particular test bench.

The test suite analysis tool within Verification Navigator offers a facility to create lists of results files and then perform various comparisons and isolate any differences. Figure 12-6 shows pictorially how the 2 results files are related to each other and the calculation that needs to be made to extract the value of the difference.

e.g. Difference = (merged + test_monitor2) - merged

Figure 12-7 shows how the above 'difference calculation' is setup using the Compare facility in Verification Navigator.

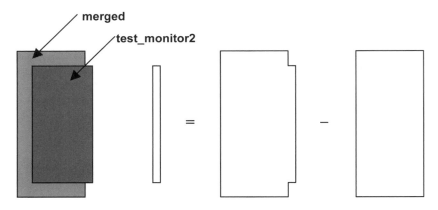

Difference = (merged + test_monitor2) – merged

Figure 12-6

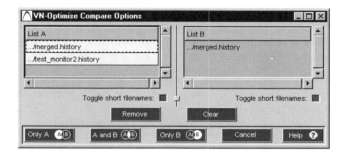

Figure 12-7

As shown in Figure 12-7 there are 3 buttons (labelled *Only A*, *A and B* and *Only B*) that enable various types of calculations to be performed between the results files that appear in List A and List B. In this particular example the *Only A* button is clicked, as it is the difference, after subtracting List B from List A, which is required. When any of the 3 buttons are clicked a series of calculations are performed on the two sets of results files, and the global results reported to the user. Figure 12-8 shows how Verification Navigator identifies where the various differences exist and how this information is conveyed graphically to the user. A row of tabs labelled with the coverage measurements (i.e. Statement, Branch, Condition, Toggle and Path) can be selected individually if a user requires more specific details.

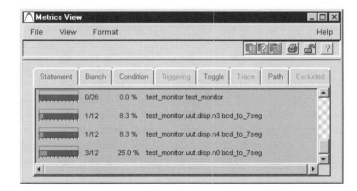

Figure 12-8

The first line entry, in Figure 12-8, shows that the test bench `test_monitor2` did not execute any additional statements not executed by the `merged` test bench in the design unit named `test_monitor`. The second and third line entries show that 1 extra statement was executed by `test_monitor2` while the fourth line entry shows that 3 extra statements have been executed. (i.e. Figure 12-8 shows a summary of the incremental contribution made by test bench `test_monitor2`.)

The next step is to inspect the HDL source code and identify exactly where these particular statements are located. Using Verification Navigator this is achieved by simply clicking the appropriate line entry, which invokes a window where the corresponding HDL source code is displayed as in Figure 12-9.

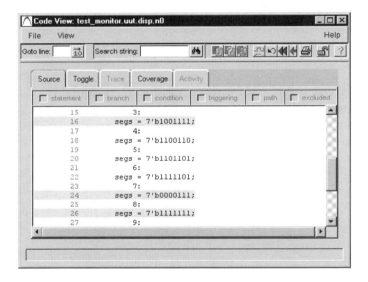

Figure 12-9

The source code listing, in Figure 12-9, highlights the 3 lines (i.e. lines 16, 24 and 26) that have been executed by the `test_monitor2` test bench. Using this information the final step is to optimize the effectiveness of one of the original test benches to include additional vectors that execute these lines of code. In this particular example it means changing any of the 2 test benches (i.e. `test_monitor1` or `test_monitor5`) that were merged to produce the compact test bench file `merged.history`

IDENTIFYING TEST BENCHES FOR ECO

In a number of situations there is a requirement to be able to identify which test bench or test benches executed a particular line of HDL code. For example when an ECO (Engineering Change Order) occurs, a verification engineer needs to know which tests need to be re-run in order to prove that these changes have not adversely affected the operation of this design unit and its interaction with other parts of the system. Using the facilities offered by Verification Navigator this task can easily be achieved by reading in the various test bench results files and then setting up a single compare list that contains all these files. This sequence is illustrated in Figure 12-10.

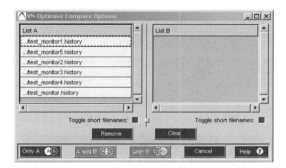

Figure 12-10

The compare button labelled Only A is clicked to invoke file processing and then the design unit that contains the HDL that has been changed is selected. This action will bring up a window, as shown in Figure 12-11, where the individual lines of source code are displayed.

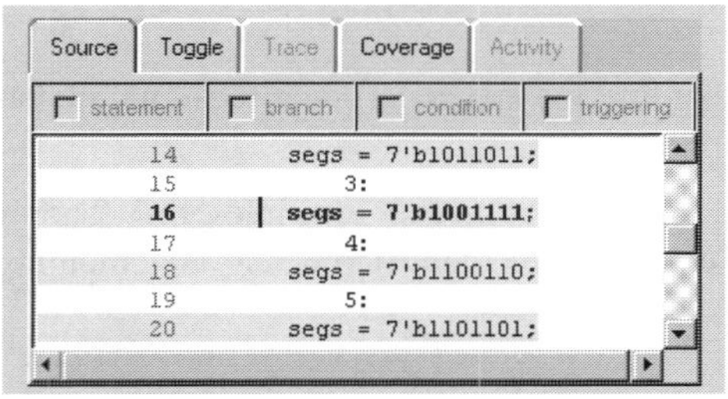

Figure 12-11

If any of the individual lines of source code are clicked the names of the test benches that executed that line of code is displayed as in Figures 12-12 and 12-13.

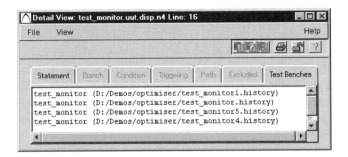

Figure 12-12

Figure 12-12 shows that line 16 in this particular design unit has been executed by test benches: `test_monitor1`, `test_monitor`, `test_monitor5` and `test_monitor4`.

Figure 12-13

Figure 12-13 shows that line 18, in this particular design unit, has only been executed by test bench: `test_monitor1`.

Although these have been fairly trivial examples they should illustrate how the relevant test benches can easily be identified when implementing engineering change orders.

Appendix A

On-Line Resources and Further Reading

This appendix gives details of how you can acquire a set of software tools and related Verilog and VHDL source files that will enable you to work through the practical exercises and case studies that appear in Appendix B thru to G. The step-by-step practical exercises and case studies have been designed to enable you quickly to acquire experience of the various coverage analysis concepts described in this manual. If you are planning to conduct an in-depth evaluation of the coverage analysis tools, then it is suggested that you do this once you have completed the exercises and developed familiarity with the products.

Although it is assumed that you will probably use the Internet to download copies of the coverage analysis tools and simulators, the software can also be obtained by contacting the appropriate vendor and requesting a compact disc.

Some useful web site addresses and newsgroups are listed below.

TransEDA	www.transeda.com
Model Technology	www.model.com
Saros Technology (UK)	www.saros.co.uk
Verilog newsgroup	comp.lang.verilog
VHDL newsgroup	comp.lang.vhdl

COVERAGE ANALYSIS TOOLS

Full-function copies of the following front-end design tools are available from TransEDA's web site for evaluation purposes.

www.transeda.com/download.html

All the tools operate on the most popular range of engineering platforms including: SUN Solaris, HP Unix, Linux and Windows 2000/NT.

Verification Navigator

Verification Navigator is a comprehensive verification environment that contains a set of tools designed to provide:

- code coverage analysis (i.e. VN-Cover),

- finite state machine (FSM) coverage analysis (i.e. VN-Cover FSM Analyzer),

- property checking (i.e. VN-Property DX),

- test suite management and analysis (i.e. VN-Optimize).

All the tools are integrated in an easy-to-use graphical user interface that supports Verilog, VHDL and dual-language designs as well as working with the industry's leading simulators.

Design Rule Checker

The name of the design rule checker available from TransEDA is VN-Check. It is supplied with the following five comprehensive and extensible design rule databases which can be used to validate Verilog or VHDL source files.

- Best Practices

- OpenMORE

- RMM (Reuse Methodology Manual)

- Portability (VHDL to Verilog or Verilog to VHDL)

- Synthesisability

VERILOG AND VHDL SIMULATORS

Verification Navigator and State Navigator coverage analysis products have been designed to support the following leading-edge simulators.

Verilog

Verilog-XL	Cadence Design Systems
NC-Verilog	Cadence Design Systems
Verilog-VCS	Synopsys Inc
ModelSim	Model Technology

VHDL

Leapfrog	Cadence Design Systems
VSS	Synopsys Inc
ModelSim	Model Technology

If you already own one of these simulators all you need to commence your evaluation is the appropriate coverage analysis tool (i.e. Verification Navigator) and the related set of Verilog and/or VHDL source files.

ModelSim Simulator

An evaluation copy of ModelSim Special Edition (SE) that operates on SUN Solaris, HP 700, RS6000, Windows-95, Windows-98, Windows-NT or Windows-2000 platforms can be requested from Model Technology's software download page on their web site at: www.model.com/sales/qualify.html

VERILOG SOURCE FILES

The set of Verilog files, in 'zip' format, that are used in the case study and worked examples described in Appendix B and C can be obtained from TransEDA's web site:

www.transeda.com/vmm/

VHDL SOURCE FILES

The set of VHDL files, in 'zip' format, that are used in the case study and worked examples described in Appendix D can be obtained from TransEDA's web site:

www.transeda.com/vmm/

REFERENCES FOR FURTHER READING

Reuse Methodology Manual for System-on-a-chip Designs

Authors: Michael Keating and Pierre Bricaud

Published by Kluwer Academic Publishers

ISBN 0-7923-8558-6

Writing Test benches - Functional Verification of HDL Models

Author: Janick Bergeron

Published by Kluwer Academic Publishers

ISBN 0-7923-7766-4

HDL Chip Design

Author: Douglas J. Smith

Published by Doone Publications

ISBN 0-9651934-3-8

Appendix B

HDL Checking

Worked Examples

Although TransEDA's design rule checking tools will operate on various platforms with different types of simulators, the following assumptions have been made in order to simplify the number of steps in this worked example and case study.

• The platform used is Windows, preferably Windows-NT.

If you are using a different platform than the one listed above, please contact TransEDA for an alternative set of instructions on how to run the worked example.

GETTING ORGANIZED

It is assumed that VN-Check or Verification Navigator with the optional VN-Check module has been installed on your system according to the vendor's instructions; that the environment variables and search paths have been set up and that the software operates correctly. If this is not the case please contact the vendor's technical support department for further assistance before going any further.

Although this exercise makes use of a couple of Verilog source files located on TransEDA's web site at: www.transeda.com/vmm/ you may prefer to substitute your own Verilog or VHDL files.

If you encounter any problems in obtaining the source files please contact TransEDA at the following e-mail address.

vmm@transeda.com

STARTING THE RULE-BASED CHECKER

Create a working directory (e.g. my-verilog or my-vhdl) on your system and then unpack the set of files that you obtained in the above step into that area. Alternatively, you can copy your own Verilog or VHDL files into this directory.

If you are using VN-Check in a standalone mode it can be invoked by entering the following text string.

```
C:\my-verilog> vncheck
```

If you are using VN-Check within the Verification Navigator environment (i.e. as an additional optional module) it can be invoked by entering the following text string and then clicking the button labelled Rule Checker on the main flowchart.

```
C:\my-verilog> vnavigator
```

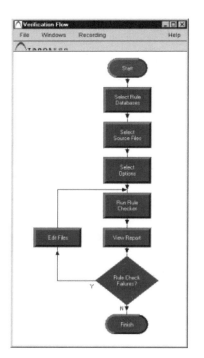

Either of the above actions will bring up a flowchart (as shown in Figure B-1) that shows graphically the major parts of the rule-based checker and how the various parts relate to each other.

The blue colored buttons in the flowchart are organised to guide a user quickly and easily through the following steps.

• Selecting a rule database

• Selecting the source files

• Selecting the run options

• Running the rule-based checker

• Viewing the results

• Editing the source files

Figure B-1

Each of the above steps are described in detail on the following pages.

SELECTING A RULE DATABASE

Move the cursor into the main window labelled VN-Check and click the tab labelled Verilog or VHDL to define which HDL design language you want to use. Access to the set of rule databases, that are supplied with VN-Check, is achieved by clicking the second button labelled Select Rule Databases on the flowchart. This will bring up a window where you can select one or more of the supplied rule databases (as shown in Figure B-2 and B-3). For this particular example the RMM.rdb or BestPractices.rdb rule database is probably the best choice to make.

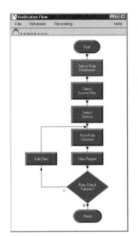
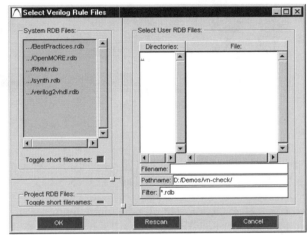

Figure B-2	**Figure B-3**

Click the OK button once you have made your choice. The next step is to select which source files you want to check against the rule databases that were chosen in the above step.

SELECTING THE SOURCE FILES

Click the third button on the flowchart labelled Select Source Files. This action will bring up a browser window where you can navigate to the directory that contains your source files. If you invoked VN-Check in the working directory where your source files are located then the source files should be immediately visible. If you are using the demonstration Verilog files, that are available at TransEDA's web site, then select the source file labelled verilog-bad.v Although this particular source file will compile and run correctly it does contain a number of coding, style and documentation problems that will be detected by VN-Check. Figures B-4 and B-5 highlights the areas on the GUI (Graphical User Interface) where the source file(s) are selected.

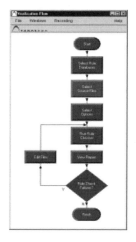

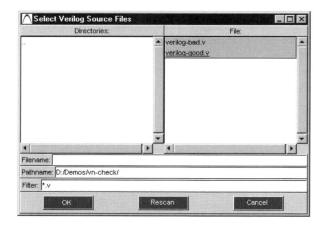

Figure B-4   Figure B-5

SELECTING THE RUN OPTIONS

Click the Select Options button - the fourth button on the flowchart. Move the cursor into the main window labelled VN-Check and click the button labelled Run Options to bring up a small window that lists the options available at run-time. For this particular example the options can be left unchecked as shown in Figure B-6. Click the OK button to dismiss the window.

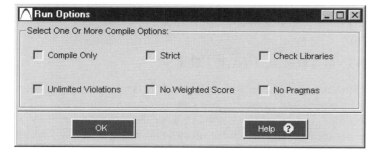

Figure B-6

RUNNING THE RULE-BASED CHECKER

Click the Run Rule Checker button - the fifth button on the flowchart to bring up the Analyze Log window. As each file is analyzed a report is generated and sent to this window to show how many violations have been detected by VN-Check. The violations are categorised into coding, style, documentation and naming problems. The window can be closed by clicking the Dismiss button once you have familiarised yourself with the content of the report.

VIEWING THE RESULTS

Click the View Report button - the sixth button on the flowchart to bring up the Select Report Files window. This action will open up a browser window where you can navigate to the directory that contains your report file. If you invoked VN-Check in the working directory where your source files are located then the report file should be immediately visible. If you have used the demonstration Verilog files, that are available at TransEDA's web site, and providing you have not altered any of the default options for VN-Check you should see a file labelled `VN-Check-vl.rpt` Highlight this particular file by clicking on its name and then press the OK button. This action will update the two main windows that are labelled Results Navigator and VN-Check with the information as shown in Figure B-7.

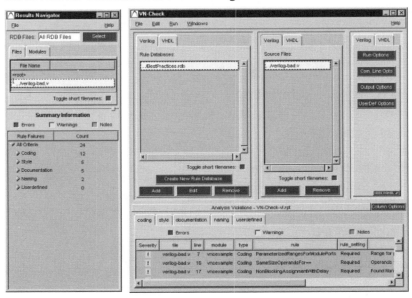

Figure B-7

The information displayed in the Results Navigator panel can be expanded by clicking the triangular buttons (as shown in Figure B-8 and B-9) to reveal the violation details for the coding, style, documentation and naming problems.

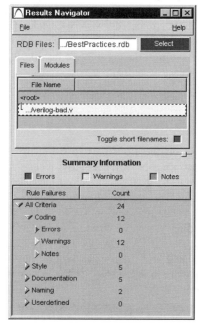

Figure B-8

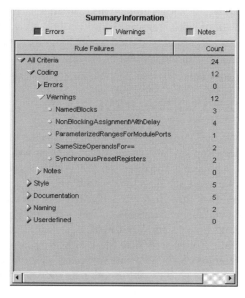

Figure B-9

In this particular example there are 12 warnings that relate to coding problems that have been violated in the Best Practices rule database.

They are:

• Named Blocks	3
• Non Blocking Assignments With Delay	4
• Parameterized Ranges For Module Ports	1
• Same Size Operands For ==	2
• Synchronous Preset Registers	2

More information about each violation can be obtained by clicking on each line in the Summary Information panel. For example, try clicking on the entry that relates to the

Named Blocks violation. Each time you do this the relevant line of code that contains a problem will be highlighted in the VN-Check window. (e.g. line 15, 24 and 32.) At the same time the lower portion of the VN-Check window will display detailed information about each violation. This is shown in Figure B-10.

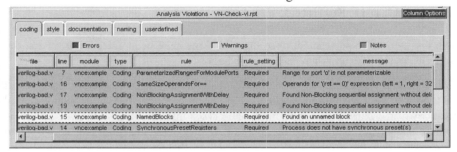

Figure B-10

The named block violation is probably fairly easy to understand as it refers to a *begin* and *end* block that does not contain a name or label next to the *begin* keyword. Naming a block assists a designer to locate problems during the debugging phase and also makes code more readable and easier to maintain.

Some of the other problems identified by VN-Check relate to:

(a) not having a delay value specified in a non-blocking assignment,
(b) a module port that contains absolute values rather than parameterized values,
(c) mismatch in the width of operands on the left and right side of an assignment,
(d) synchronous presets missing within a register.

As there are a huge number of rules in each rule-database, a designer may require further supportive information in order to understand why a rule has been broken and more importantly how to fix the problem in the HDL source code. A database querying facility is built into VN-Check to enable a user to instantly obtained details about any rule violations. As shown in Figure B-11, this is achieved by clicking the right-hand mouse button over a highlighted rule violation to reveal a drop-down menu.

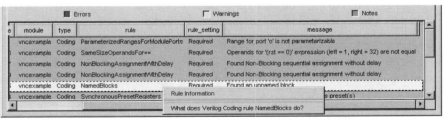

Figure B-11

Whenever an entry in the drop-down menu is clicked a detailed explanation window is brought up to provide further guidance for the designer.

EDITING THE SOURCE FILES

The last step to be performed, once the violations have been detected, is to edit the original source files and then re-run VN-Check.

There are two ways to invoke VN-Check's in-built editor. The first and most obvious method is to click the button labelled Edit Files on the flowchart. The second method (as shown in Figure B-12) is to move the cursor into the main VN-Check window (where the source code for the file that is currently being analyzed is displayed) and then right-click the mouse button over the line that contains the problem. Either method will invoke a text editor as shown in Figure B-13.

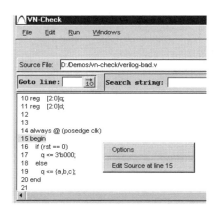 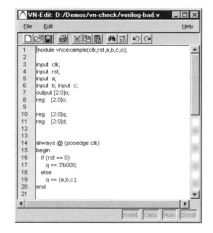

Figure B-12   **Figure B-13**

If a designer prefers to use a different text editor (e.g. VI or EMACS) then this can be achieved by altering the following parameter in vnavigator.par

```
gui editor <editor_name>
```

Please refer to Chapter 3 of VN-Check's on-line manual for details of the range of editors supported and the corresponding syntax to be used in the above command string.

Once you have completed this simple exercise you should be able to use VN-Check to validate your own personal or project related HDL source files.

Appendix C

Verilog Coverage Analysis

Worked Examples

Although TransEDA's coverage analysis tools will operate on various platforms with different types of simulators, the following assumptions have been made in order to simplify the number of steps in these worked examples and case studies.

- The platform used is Windows, preferably Windows-NT.

- The simulator used is ModelSim version 5.5 or later.

If you are using a different platform or simulator than the ones listed above, please contact TransEDA for an alternative set of instructions on how to run the worked example and case study.

GETTING ORGANIZED

It is assumed that Verification Navigator version 2002.03 or later and ModelSim have been installed on your system according to the vendors' instructions; that the environment variables and search paths have been set up and that the software operates correctly. If this is not the case please contact the vendors' technical support department for further assistance before going any further.

The various Verilog design files, configuration files and associated batch files needed for the case study can be obtained as a single file in 'zip' format from TransEDA's web site at: www.transeda.com/vmm/

If you encounter any problems in obtaining the 'zip' file please contact TransEDA at the following e-mail address.

vmm@transeda.com

DIRECTORY AND FILE STRUCTURE

Create a directory (e.g. my-verilog) on your system and then unpack the complete set of files that you obtained in the above step into that area. Make sure the directory contains the following files and the filenames and suffix are correct.

```
addr_decoder.v
bcd_to_7seg.v
clock_div.v
cpu.v
data_file.v
digital_monitor.v
display.v
prog_mem.v
test_monitor.v
    // This is the test bench
circuit.f
    // List of the Verilog files in the design
data_bus.var
    // Variable-trace definition file
doit.modelsim.bat
    // Command line batch file
vnavigator.par
    // Parameter file for Verification Navigator
```

Command Line Batch File

A command line batch file is supplied which can be used to automate the process of analyzing and instrumenting the Verilog source files, running the simulation and collecting the activity-data for the history file. To assist you in understanding the operation of this stage, each line of the batch file (doit.modelsim.bat) is annotated below.

```
1.  vlib work_lib
2.  vmap work_lib ./work_lib
3.  vmap work work_lib
4.  vlog test_montor.v
```

```
5.    vnvlog -- -f circuit.f
6.    vnsim -- test_monitor
7.    vnresults
```

Lines 1 to 3 create a library to hold the design files that will be analyzed and instrumented. As it is not normal practice to instrument the test bench this is compiled outside of the coverage analysis tool using the command given by Line 4. The Verilog source files that make up the complete design that need to be analyzed and instrumented are listed in the `circuit.f` file. This information is passed to VN-Cover by the command given on Line 5. The syntax for this particular command is given below.

```
vnvlog <VN options> -- < simulator options>
```

Although it is normal practice to use a file to hold a list of the Verilog source files that are used in the design, the names of the source files could be passed to VN-Cover on separate lines as shown below.

```
vnvlog   addr_decoder.v    REM   Line 5a
vnvlog   bcd_to_7seg.v     REM   Line 5b
   etc...
```

Line 6 specifies the name of the test bench or top-level module (e.g. test_monitor) and runs a normal Verilog simulation to collect the activity-data for the complete design. This information is written to a history file that has a default name of `vnavigator.index`. Line 7 is a post-processing stage that creates a series of text files that gives detailed coverage information for each instance of each module in the design. These files can be viewed with a simple text editor

Parameter File (Global and Local)

Verification Navigator uses a parameter file called `vnavigator.par` to define how the coverage analysis tool is used and the types of coverage measurements applied to your design. A global parameter file, that is located in the area where you installed the coverage analysis software, defines all the default settings for Verification Navigator. A local parameter, that is located in your working area, enables the default settings to be overridden. An explanation of the contents of the local parameter file is listed below.

```
1.    all simulator modelsim_verilog_nt
2.    vnvlog statement
3.    vnvlog branch
4.    vnvlog path
```

```
5.  vnvlog condition
6.  vnvlog toggle
7.  vnvlog ports
8.  vnvlog activity
```

Line 1 sets Verification Navigator to use the ModelSim Verilog simulator running on a Windows-NT platform. Lines 2 to 8 define the types of coverage analysis measurements to be instrumented during the HDL code analysis phase.

COLLECTING COVERAGE RESULTS

Make sure you are positioned in the directory that you created to hold the Verilog source files. Invoke the command line batch file by entering the following text string.

```
C:\my-verilog> doit.modelsim.bat
```

This action will automatically invoke the VN-Cover part of Verification Navigator and carry out the following steps.

- Analyze and Instrument the Verilog source files.

- Call the ModelSim simulator to collect coverage information.

- Output a results file containing the activity-data.

- Produce a series of text files containing detailed coverage information.

The name of the results file is: `vnavigator.index` which is located in the default sub-directory: `vnavigator_results`

VIEWING COVERAGE RESULTS

There are two ways to view the detailed coverage information that was produced by the command line batch file. You can either inspect the contents of the coverage files with a text editor or use the GUI (graphical user interface) that is available within VN-Cover. This worked example will make use of the graphical user interface which can be invoked by entering the following text string.

```
C:\my-verilog> vnavigator
```

This action will bring up a top-level flowchart, as shown in Figure C-1, to guide you through the various tools that are available within Verification Navigator's verification environment.

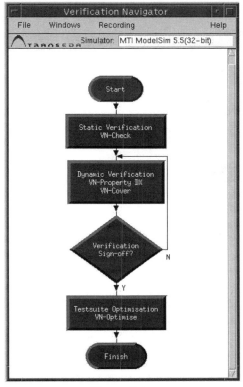

Figure C-1

The first button will invoke the Static Verification tool know as VN-Check. Further details on this particular tool can be found in Appendix B.

The second button will invoke the Dynamic Verification tool known as VN-Cover. You should click this button to bring up another flowchart, as shown in Figure C-2 below. This flowchart is known as the Verification Flow and is designed to guide you through the various parts of the Dynamic Verification tool.

The third button will cause a window to be displayed that shows how many of the design units or modules have satisfied the user specified sign-off criteria.

The fourth button will invoke the Testsuite Optimisation tool know as VN-Optimise. Further information on this particular tool can be found in Chapter 12.

The Verification Flow flowchart, as shown in Figure C-2, is used to allow you to interact graphically with VN-Cover to create libraries, select the design files that you want to instrument and set up communication with your chosen simulator. As we have already generated the results file using the command line script (doit.modelsim.bat) we can skip this stage and move on to inspecting the coverage results.

Click the Results button - the sixth button on the flowchart.

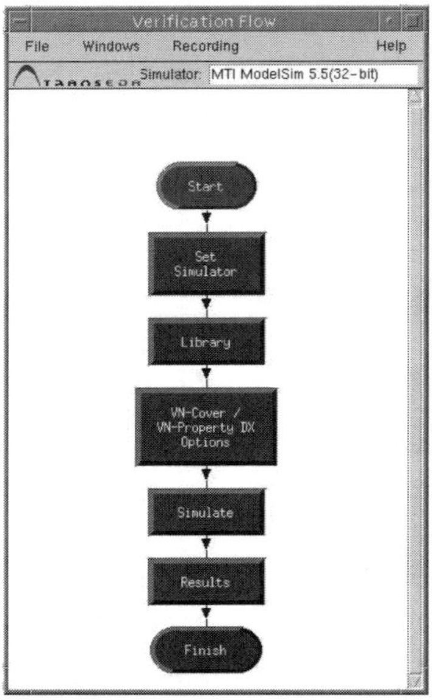

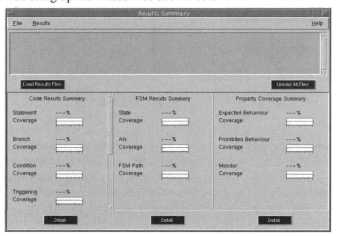

Figure C-2

This action will bring up the window as shown below.

Figure C-3

Click the Load Results Files button to display the results files that are available.

Select the file labelled `vnavigator.index` by clicking the corresponding entry in the Results File(s) pop-up window. This action will load the requested results file into Verification Navigator's internal database area. A summary of the coverage that has been achieved is displayed in the Results Summary window.

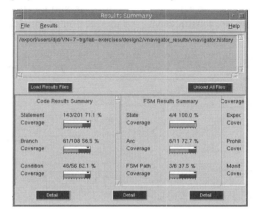

Figure C-4

Clicking the Detail button, at the base of the Results Summary window, will enable you to obtain detailed information about coverage in specific parts of the design. The action of clicking the Detail button will cause the display screen to change and become populated with the set of six windows as shown in Figure C-5.

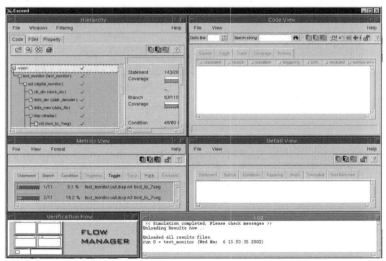

Figure C-5

The Flow Manager window is really an iconised version of the Verification Flow window and can be used as a way to return to the main flow if you need to repeat the instrumentation or simulation phases.

The right-hand section of the Hierarchy window, as shown in Figure C-6, shows a summary of the coverage measurements for the section of the design's hierarchy that is currently selected. At the moment the whole of the design's hierarchy has been selected so what is indicated is a global summary for the whole of the design.

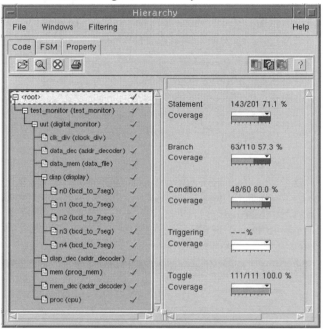

Figure C-6

As you move around the design by clicking the appropriate module or instance in the hierarchy viewer the summary values change to reflect the coverage at that particular level. The information displayed in the Hierarchy window enables you to identify quickly the areas of your design that have poor coverage. An inter-window communication process links the Hierarchy window with the Metric View window (as shown in Figure C-7) and enables you to inspect specific coverage metric values for individual modules or instances. Although the Hierarchy window is basically a static window, the Metric View window is dynamic and enables the individual values for the coverage measurements to be displayed by clicking the appropriate metric tab located along the top edge of the window.

Figure C-7 shows an example of how the coverage information is displayed when the Statement tab has been selected.

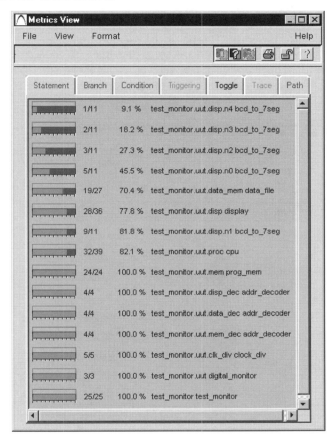

Figure C-7

Modules or instances that have poor coverage are listed first and color-coded to assist you in identifying the areas of the design that need your attention. In this particular example, there is poor coverage with the bcd_to_7seg module-instance which indicates that extra test vectors need to be added to the test bench. At this stage you can try clicking some of the other metric tabs along the top edge of the window to ascertain the amount of coverage that has been achieved for Branch, Condition, Path, Toggle and Signal-Tracing. Please refer to Chapter 6 for details on how to interpret each of these coverage measurements.

A Code View window communicates with the Metric View window and is used to locate the source code for each instance. Figure C-8 shows how the Verilog code is displayed in the Code View window. The example here relates to the ALU code for the 'cpu' contained in the 'proc' module. Various lines of code are highlighted indicating inadequate coverage. This particular example highlights the problems with inadequate statement coverage by identifying the lines of code that have a zero execution count. You can examine the problems with the other coverage measurements by clicking the appropriate tab across the top edge of the Code View window.

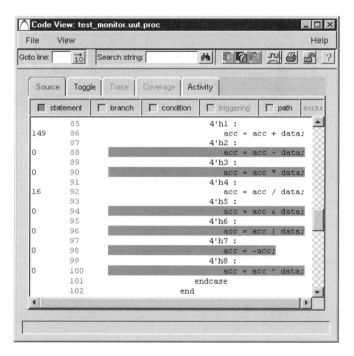

Figure C-8

It is a simple matter to locate and identify statements that have zero execution counts. However some of the more powerful coverage measurements may require further explanation in order to identify exactly what is wrong with a section of Verilog code. A Detailed View window is available for this purpose. If you click on a particular line of code, the Detailed Code View window will be invoked to display in-depth information. The resultant action that you need to take will probably involve altering the test vectors supplied by the test bench or modifying a section of Verilog in the corresponding source file.

Figures C-9 to C-12 show how the Detailed Code window reports problems associated with branch coverage, condition coverage, path coverage and signal trace coverage respectively.

The worked example described in this appendix should help you in developing some basic experience and confidence in using a coverage tool. It is suggested that once you have completed this simple example you try using the coverage tools with one of your own projects.

If required, additional practical exercises can be obtained from TransEDA and can also be found in the 'example' directory where Verification Navigator was installed on your system.

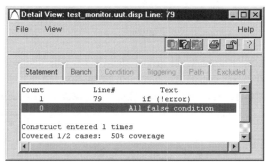

Figure C-9

The error reported in Figure C-9 indicates that the branch at line 79 has always been taken because the value of !error has always been true. (i.e. logic 0.) An additional vector is needed in the test bench to set !error=1 and thus increase the branch coverage to 100%.

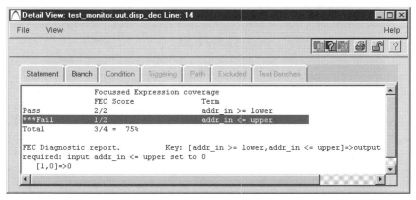

Figure C-10

Figure C-10 indicates that one of the terms in the complex 'if' statement on line 14 has failed to control the expression. Please refer to Chapter 6 for details on how to interpret the diagnostic messages for focussed expression coverage.

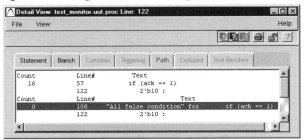

Figure C-11

The report shown by Figure C-11 gives details of which combinations of paths through the 'if' and 'case' constructs have not been covered.

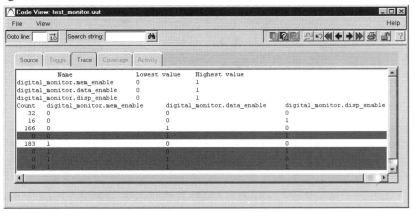

Figure C-12

One useful coverage measurement that was described in Chapter 6 is variable-trace. This technique is particularly useful at the functional or black box testing stage. A data file, which is normally formatted as a simple text file, is used to define the names of the signals/variables to be traced. If you inspect the contents of the file `data_bus.var` you can see the signals that have been traced. In this example the internal data bus drivers have been traced to ascertain if more than one driver is active simultaneously. The lines that are highlighted in Figure C-12 indicate the situation when more than one driver is driving the bus. As each of the highlighted lines are indicating a zero execution count, this means that the situation where more than one driver has driven the bus has never occurred.

Appendix D

VHDL Coverage Analysis

Worked Examples

In this section we will run coverage analysis on a simple VHDL example. The software we will use is Verification Navigator 2002.03 from TransEDA. At the time of going to print this was the only commercially available general purpose coverage analysis tool for VHDL. The following environment will be used:

- Operating system: Unix (Sun Solaris 2.7)

- VHDL simulator: ModelSim 5.5 from Model Technology Inc.

Verification Navigator supports a number of simulators and operating systems, if your configuration is different please contact TransEDA for an alternative set of instructions on how to run the worked example and case study.

GETTING ORGANIZED

It is assumed that Verification Navigator and ModelSim have both been installed according to the vendor's instructions and that the necessary environment (PATH etc.) has been set up to run both tools. If this is not the case, please contact the relevant vendor for technical support before going any further.

The various files necessary to run this case study can be obtained as a single 'zip' file (for Windows) or 'tar' file (for Unix) from the TransEDA web site at:

www.transeda.com/vmm/

If you encounter any problems in obtaining the 'zip' file please contact TransEDA at the following e-mail address:

vmm@transeda.com

DIRECTORY AND FILE STRUCTURE

Create a new directory on your system, and then unpack the 'tar' file into that directory. The directory should now contain the following files:

Design and test bench VHDL files:

```
alu.vhd
asic.vhd
controller_a.vhd
controller_e.vhd
numeric_bit.vhd
test_asic.vhd
```

Test vector file (read by test_asic.vhd):

```
test.vec
```

Verification Navigator options file:

```
vnavigator.par
```

Batch script file:

```
doit.modelsim
```

GETTING THE RESULTS

It is possible to run Verification Navigator completely from the graphical user interface (GUI), although in this case study we will run a batch script. Batch operation is commonly used for large designs because it is far easier to write a script once to be re-used many times. In this case study our batch script is called doit.modelsim and its contents is as follows:

```
1.  vnlib   -create coverlib=./vlib
2.  vnlib   -setwork coverlib
3.  vnvhdl -noinstrument numeric_bit.vhd
4.  vnvhdl alu.vhd
5.  vnvhdl controller_e.vhd
6.  vnvhdl -declaration\
        controller_e.vhd controller_a.vhd
7.  vnvhdl asic.vhd
8.  vnvhdl -noinstrument test_asic.vhd
9.  vnsim   -run 550ns test_asic_configuration
```

The vnlib commands create libraries and set up logical names, and are analogous to the ModelSim vlib and vmap commands. The first command creates a library in the directory called ./vlib with the VHDL logical name 'coverlib'. The 'work' library is set to be 'coverlib' by the second command.

The vnvhdl commands instrument (add extra VHDL to collect the coverage analysis) and compile the VHDL files. The standard VHDL compilation order rules apply, just as they would for the ModelSim vcom command. The design is compiled bottom up and in the case of controller_e.vhd and controller_a.vhd the entity is compiled before the architecture. The separate entity file is also listed as a declarations file when processing the architecture so all the port types are known. The -noinstrument switch is used to suppress coverage collection on the package file and the test bench. The coverage options for the other VHDL files are defined by the options file vnavigator.par, although these can also be specified on the command line.

The final command in the batch script (vnsim) runs the simulation and collects coverage information. This is analogous to the ModelSim vsim command and runs your normal simulation test bench. The optional -run switch defines how long the simulation is to be run for. If there is more that one test bench for the design the vnsim line would be repeated for each test bench, taking care to choose a different results file name in each case.

To run the batch script the command is:

```
$ ./doit.modelsim
```

If your environment has been set up correctly this will create the results file vmm.res. This file is best reviewed using the graphical user interface, although a batch command to create man-readable results files does exist.

To start the graphical user interface the command is:

```
$ vnavigator &
```

This action will bring up a top-level flowchart, as shown in Figure D-1, to guide you through the various tools that are available within Verification Navigator's verification environment.

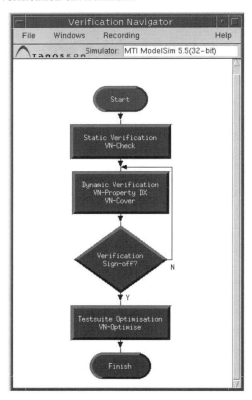

Figure D-1

The first button will invoke the Static Verification tool know as VN-Check. Further details on this particular tool can be found in Appendix B.

The second button will invoke the Dynamic Verification tool known as VN-Cover. You should click this button to bring up another flowchart, as shown in Figure D-2 below. This flowchart is known as the Verification Flow and is designed to guide you through the various parts of the Dynamic Verification tool.

The third button will cause a window to be displayed that shows how many of the design units or modules have satisfied the user specified sign-off criteria.

The fourth button will invoke the Testsuite Optimisation tool know as VN-Optimise. Further information on this particular tool can be found in Chapter 12.

The Verification Flow flowchart, as shown in Figure D-2, is used to allow you to interact graphically with VN-Cover to create libraries, select the design files that you want to instrument and set up communication with your chosen simulator. As we have already generated the results file using the command line script (doit.modelsim) we can skip this stage and move on to inspecting the coverage results.

Click the Results button - the sixth button on the flowchart.

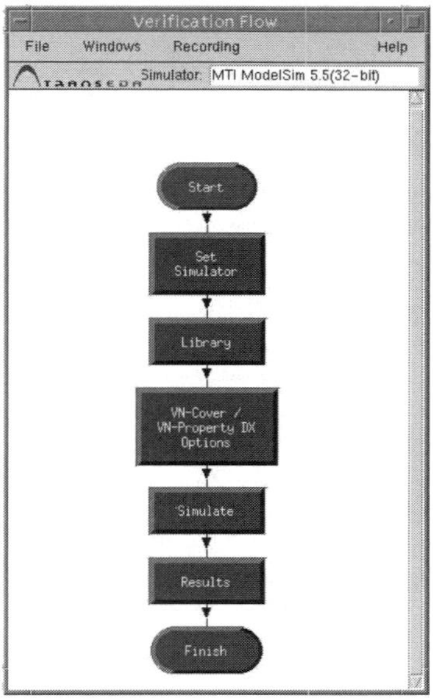

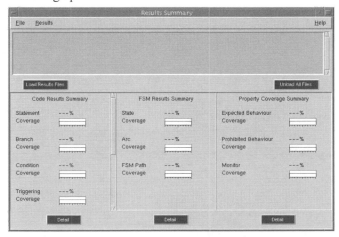

Figure D-2

This action will bring up the window as shown below.

Figure D-3

Click the Load Results Files button to display the list of results files that are available to you.

Select the file labelled vnavigator.index by clicking the corresponding entry in the Results File(s) pop-up window. This action will load the requested results file into Verification Navigator's internal database area. A summary of the coverage that has been achieved is displayed in the Results Summary window.

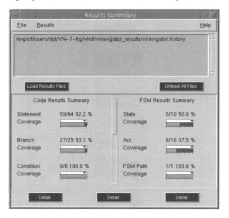

Figure D-4

Clicking the Detail button, at the base of the Results Summary window, will enable you to obtain detailed information about coverage in specific parts of the design. The action of clicking the Detail button will cause the display screen to change and become populated with the set of six windows as shown in Figure D-5.

Figure D-5

The Flow Manager window is really an iconised version of the Verification Flow window and can be used as a way to return to the main flow if you need to repeat the instrumentation or simulation phases.

The right-hand section of the Hierarchy window, as shown in Figure D-6, shows a summary of the coverage measurements for the section of the design's hierarchy that is currently selected. At the moment the whole of the design's hierarchy has been selected so what is indicated is a global summary for the whole of the design.

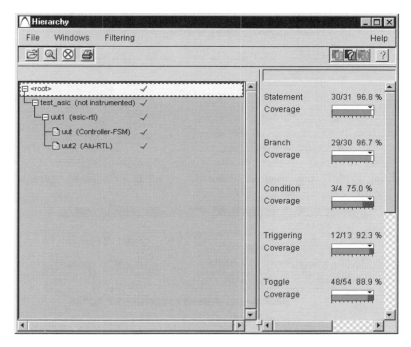

Figure D-6

The Hierarchy window shows the cumulative coverage for all the measurements for either the whole of the design hierarchy or a part of it. To see the figures for part of the hierarchy click on the name of the instance at the top of the sub-tree you are interested in. If the overall coverage shown in the Hierarchy window is not acceptable the next step is to investigate the problems. The Metrics View window, shown in Figure D-7, makes this easy by listing, for every coverage measurement, all the design instances in the order of worst coverage through to best coverage. This makes it quick and easy to find the instances with coverage problems.

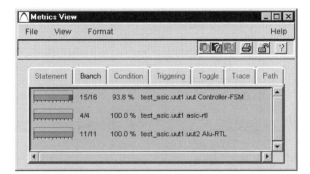

Figure D-7

The next step is to click on an instance in the Metrics window which you are interested in (for example `test_asic.uut1.uut`). This displays the VHDL source code for that instance in the Code View window with color-coded highlighting to show the coverage problems. Figure D-8 shows an example of the Code View window.

Figure D-8

If more detail is required on any coverage problem you can click on the color-coded line to pop up the Detail View window. Figure D-9 shows the branch Detail View window produced by clicking on line 37 of the Code View. The Detail View window shows that one branch of the 'case' statement has not been executed.

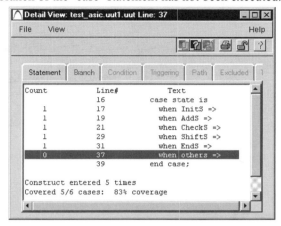

Figure D-9

Figure D-10 shows the condition coverage detail created by clicking on line 32 in the Code View window. In this example, the expression has two inputs, and input RTB has not uniquely controlled the expression to logical 1. The report lists the test pattern required to complete the coverage on that expression (STB = 0, RTB = 1).

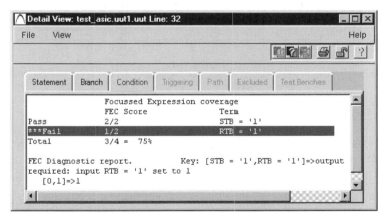

Figure D-10

The detailed toggle coverage information is obtained by pressing on the Toggle tab in the Code View window. Figure D-11 shows an example of this for instance test_asic.uut1.uut2. In this example only one signal has not been toggled by the test bench and is therefore highlighted.

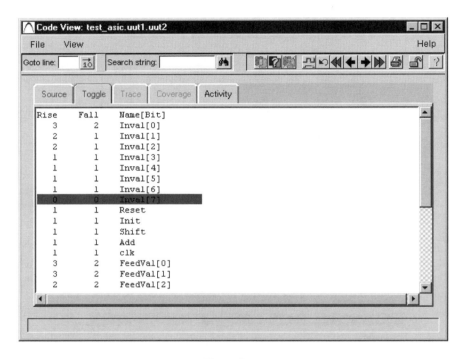

Figure D-11

We have worked through the basic principles of collecting and viewing coverage analysis results for a VHDL design. Having identified the coverage analysis problems it is up to you as the designer or verification engineer to decide if the missing coverage is significant and if so how to add extra test patterns to test the uncovered code.

If required additional practical exercises can be obtained from TransEDA and can also be found in the 'example' directory where Verification Navigator was installed on your system.

Appendix E

FSM Coverage

Worked Examples

As this appendix uses the same set of Verilog files as Appendix C you should refer to that appendix for instructions on how to obtain and download the files.

DIRECTORY AND FILE STRUCTURE

Create a directory (e.g. my-fsm) on your system and then unpack the complete set of files that you obtained in the above step into that area. Make sure the directory contains the following files and that the filenames and suffix are correct.

```
addr_decoder.v
bcd_to_7seg.v
clock_div.v
cpu.v
data_file.v
digital_monitor.v
display.v
prog_mem.v
data_bus.var
test_monitor.v      // This is the test bench
circuit.f           // Verilog files in the design
doit.fsm.bat        // Command line batch file
vnavigator.par      // Parameter file
```

Command Line Batch File

A command line batch file (called doit.fsm.bat) is supplied which can be used to automate the process of analyzing and instrumenting the Verilog source files, running the simulation and collecting the activity-data for the results file. To assist you in understanding the operation of this stage, each line of the batch file is explained below.

```
1. vnlib   -verilog -delete work_lib
2. vnlib   -verilog -create my-work=./my-work
3. vnlib   -verilog -setwork my-work
4. vnvlog -fsmstate -fsmarc -fsmpath -- -f circut.f
5. vnsim   -fsmpath -- test_monitor
6. vnresults -format detail \
              -design_units test_monitor.uut.proc
```

Lines 1 to 3 create a new library to hold the design files that will be analyzed and instrumented. The Verilog source files that make up the complete design that need to be analyzed and instrumented are listed in the circuit.f file. This information is passed to VN-Cover by the command given on Line 4 together with the options to collect state, arc and path coverage for any finite state machines that are contained in any of the Verilog files.

Line 5 specifies the name of the test bench or top-level module (e.g. test_monitor) and runs a normal Verilog simulation to collect the activity-data for the complete design. Line 5 also specifies that FSM path coverage should be evaluated during the simulation The information is written to a results file that has a default name of vnavigator.index. Line 6 is a post-processing stage that creates a text file (from the FSM results file) that gives detailed coverage information for the instances specified in the design_units options. In this particular example only the proc instance contains a finite state machine, so to save time this is the only instance that is included in the design_units options. A simple text editor can be used to inspect the contents of test_monitor.uut.proc.txt and determine the amount of arc, state and path coverage for the FSM in cpu.v.

COLLECTING COVERAGE RESULTS

Make sure you are positioned in the directory that you created to hold the Verilog source files. Invoke the command line batch file by entering the following text string.

```
C:\my-fsm> doit.fsm.bat
```

This action will automatically invoke the VN-Cover part of Verification Navigator and carry out the following steps.

- Analyze and Instrument the Verilog source files.

- Call the ModelSim simulator to collect FSM coverage information.

- Output a results file containing the FSM activity-data.

- Produce a text file containing detailed coverage information.

The name of the results file is: `vnavigator.index` which is located in the default sub-directory: `vnavigator_results`

During the analysis phase a static verification check is performed on any finite state machine that are detected in the various Verilog source files. A number of warnings that relate to the state register that is used within the `cpu.v` file are displayed in the terminal window. For example, there are warnings about:

- no default state assignment

This message indicates that there is no default clause specified within a 'case' construct to explicitly define that the state machine should remain in the same state if none of the other conditions (that would cause it to move to another state) are detected.

- unreachable state

This message indicates that, although there is a piece of HDL code that describes a particular state within the state machine, there is no way of getting to that code from any of the other states. During the simulation phase a number of checks are made to determine the dynamic coverage on each of the extracted state machines. These checks include: FSM state coverage, FSM arc or transition coverage as well as FSM path coverage.

VIEWING COVERAGE RESULTS

There are two ways to view the detailed coverage information that was produced by the command line batch file. You can either inspect the contents of the coverage files with a text editor or use the GUI (graphical user interface) that is available within VN-Cover. This worked example will make use of the graphical user interface which can be invoked by entering the following text string.

```
C:\my-fsm> vnavigator
```

This action will bring up a top-level flowchart, as shown in Figure E-1, to guide you through the various tools that are available within Verification Navigator's verification environment.

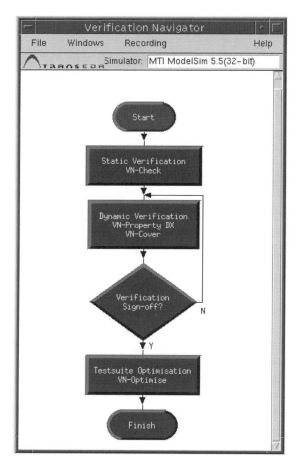

Figure E-1

The first button will invoke the Static Verification tool know as VN-Check. Further details on this particular tool can be found in Appendix B.

The second button will invoke the Dynamic Verification tool known as VN-Cover. You should click this button to bring up another flowchart, as shown in Figure E-2 below. This flowchart is known as the Verification Flow and is designed to guide you through the various parts of the Dynamic Verification tool.

The third button will cause a window to be displayed that shows how many of the design units or modules have satisfied the user specified sign-off criteria.

The fourth button will invoke the Testsuite Optimisation tool know as VN-Optimise. Further information on this particular tool can be found in Chapter 12.

The Verification Flow flowchart, as shown in Figure E-2, is used to allow you to interact graphically with VN-Cover to create libraries, select the design files that you want to instrument and set up communication with your chosen simulator. As we have already generated the results file using the command line script (doit.fsm.bat) we can skip this stage and move on to inspecting the FSM coverage results.

Click the Results button - the sixth button as shown on the following flowchart.

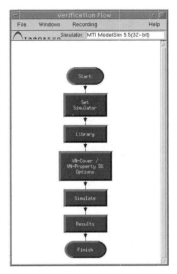

Figure E-2

This action will bring up the window as shown below.

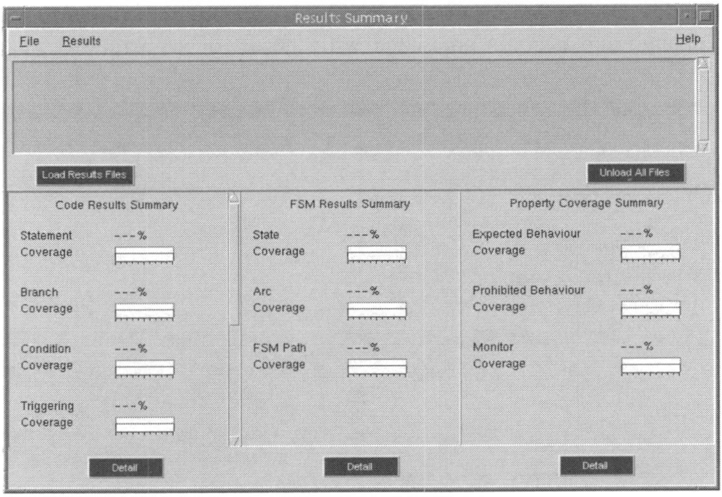

Figure E-3

Click the Load Results Files button to display the results files that are available.

Select the file labelled `vnavigator.index` by clicking the corresponding entry in the Results File(s) pop-up window. This action will load the requested results file into Verification Navigator's internal database area. A summary of the coverage that has been achieved is displayed in the Results Summary window.

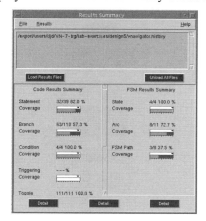

Figure E-4

Clicking the Detail button, at the base of the FSM Results Summary area of the window, will enable you to obtain detailed information about coverage in specific parts of the design. The action of clicking the Detail button will cause the display screen to change and become populated with the set of six windows as shown in Figure E-5.

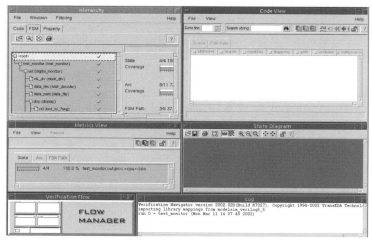

Figure E-5

The Flow Manager window is really an iconised version of the Verification Flow window and can be used as a way to return to the main flow if you need to repeat the instrumentation or simulation phases.

The right-hand section of the Hierarchy window, as shown in Figure E-6, shows a summary of the FSM coverage measurements for the section of the design's hierarchy that is currently selected. At the moment the whole of the design's hierarchy has been selected so what is indicated is a global summary for all the state machines that have been detected. As only one state machine has been detected in this design the global summary will relate to just this single state machine.

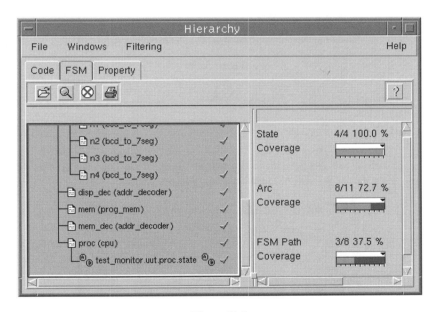

Figure E-6

As you move around the design by clicking the appropriate module or instance in the hierarchy viewer the summary values change to reflect the coverage at that particular level. The information displayed in the Hierarchy window enables you to identify quickly the state machines that have poor coverage. An inter-window communication process links the Hierarchy window with the Metrics View window (as shown in Figure E-7) and enables you to inspect specific coverage metric values for individual state machines. Although the Hierarchy window is basically a static window, the Metrics View window is dynamic and enables the individual values for FSM coverage measurements to be displayed by clicking the appropriate metric tab located along the top edge of the window.

State Coverage

For example, clicking the entry that relates to the `proc` module in the Hierarchy window will cause state coverage information to be display as shown in Figure E-7.

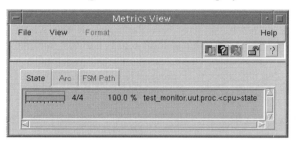

Figure E-7

Arc and Path Coverage

As shown below, arc and path coverage results for the FSM can also be obtained by clicking the appropriate tabs along the top edge of the window.

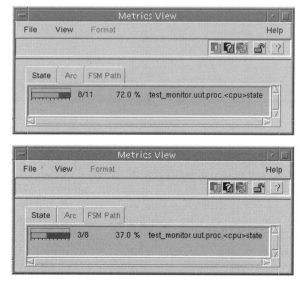

Figure E-8

State Diagram

Earlier in this appendix it was mentioned that one of the tasks conducted during the instrumentation phase was an automatic extraction process to identify any finite state machines within the HDL code. Although this information is primarily used by VN-Cover to perform a static and dynamic analysis it is also used to automatically generate a state diagram for each extracted state machines. An example of the state diagram produced by VN-Cover is shown in Figure E-9.

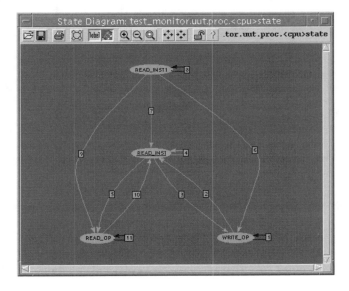

Figure E-9

The Metrics View and Code View windows communicates with the State Diagram window to enable the user to uncover the parts of the state machine that have poor coverage.

Cycle Information

Clicking the information tab labelled FSM Path in the Metric View window and then clicking the line entry (that relates to the extracted state machine) will cause the contents of the State Diagram and Code View windows to change to that shown by Figures E-9 and E-10.

The left-hand pane of the Code View window shows a list of the super-cycles that have been detected by VN-Cover and how many times each of those super-cycles have been traversed. Super-cycles that have not been exercised are shown highlighted with a red background. The pane on the right of the Code View window gives information about the sub-cycles and links that have been detected.

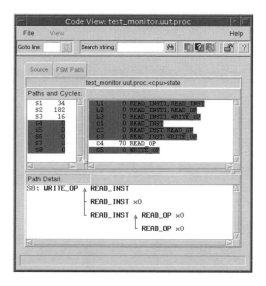

Figure E-10

The lower pane, in the Code View window, conveys detailed information about:

- how the sub-cycles relate to specific super-cycles,

- the number of times the sub-cycles have been traversed.

As some of the sub-cycles are nested within other sub-cycles this can affect the clarity of the information presented to the user. To overcome this there is a mechanism to expand or collapse the amount of information that is displayed in the Code View window. This is achieved by clicking the triangular shaped symbols to expand or contract each part of the sub-cycle.

Finally it should be noted that as you explore the FSM path coverage for the various super-cycles and sub-cycles the State Diagram is constantly updated so that you can visually see the coverage in a color-coded format. i.e. Red indicates no coverage, green indicates 100% coverage, while black indicates that coverage could not be determined.

Appendix F   *Dynamic Property Checking*

Worked Examples

RESOURCES

The various files necessary to run this case study can be obtained from the TransEDA web site at: www.transeda.com/vmm/ If you encounter any problems in obtaining these files please contact TransEDA at the e-mail address: vmm@transeda.com

DIRECTORY AND FILE STRUCTURE

Create a directory (e.g. my-pc) on your system and then unpack the complete set of files that you obtained in the above step into that area. Make sure the directory contains the following files and that the filenames and suffix are correct.

```
blackjack.v            // Blackjack card game design
blackjack_tb.v         // This is the test bench
doit.pc.bat            // Command line batch file
vnavigator.par         // Parameter file
pc_collection.spec     // Specifications file
pc_blackjack_library   // Library of properties
legal                  // Wanted properties
prohibited             // Prohibited properties
vnavigator_results     // Results directory
explain.txt            // Explanation of the design
```

Command Line Batch File

A command line batch file (called doit.pc.bat) is supplied which can be used to automate the process of analyzing and instrumenting the Verilog source files, running the simulation and collecting the activity-data for the results file.

To assist you in understanding how the results file is produced, each line of the batch file is explained below.

```
1.  vnlib   -verilog -delete my-work
2.  vnlib   -verilog -create my-work=./my-work
3.  vnlib   -verilog -setwork my-work
4.  vnpcvalidate -spec pc_collection.spec
5.  vnvlog -property -- blackjack.v blackjack_tb.v
6.  vnsim   -pc -- blackjack_tb
7.  vnpcmatch -spec pc_collection.spec
8.  vnresults -pc -spec pc_collection.spec
```

Lines 1 to 3 create a new library to hold the design files that will be analyzed and instrumented. Line 4 checks that the property specifications are syntactically correct while line 5 instruments the two design files with the property attribute to collect dynamic property coverage. Line 6 specifies the name of the test bench or top-level module (e.g. blackjack_tb) and runs a normal Verilog simulation to collect the coverage-data for the complete design. This information is written to a results file that has a default name of vnavigator.index. Line 7 performs a match between the tabular trace file (i.e. simulation results) and the properties for the design.

Line 8 is a post-processing stage that creates a set of text files from the simulation results that were matched in line 7. Two text files are produced by this step.

The first text file (called spec_legal.txt) gives a detailed list of the legal or wanted properties and how many times each property was encountered. Any properties that were not encountered will be flagged as an error.

The second text file (called spec_prohibited.txt) gives a detailed list of the unwanted or prohibited properties. None of these properties should have been encountered and should therefore have a count of zero. Any properties that have a count value of one or more are flagged as an error.

DESCRIPTION OF THE DESIGN

The design is based on modelling the behavior of the dealer in a game of Blackjack (also know as Pontoon or 21). The dealer must follow the rules of the casino: to hold on hands of 17 or more and draw another card on hands of 16 or less. If the value of the hand is greater than 21 the dealer has gone bust. Aces in the game are worth 11 or 1, picture cards (Jack, Queen or King) are worth 10. The maximum number of cards in any hand is 5.

COLLECTING COVERAGE RESULTS

Make sure you are positioned in the directory that you created to hold the Verilog source files. Invoke the command line batch file by entering the following text string.

```
C:\my-pc> doit.pc.bat
```

This action will automatically invoke the VN-Property DX part of Verification Navigator and carry out the following steps.

- Check the syntax of the properties used in the design.

- Analyze and Instrument the Verilog source files.

- Call the simulator to collect dynamic property coverage information.

- Output a results file containing dynamic property coverage information.

- Produce text file(s) containing dynamic property coverage information.

The name of the results file is: `vnavigator.index` which is located in the default sub-directory: `vnavigator_results`

VIEWING COVERAGE RESULTS

There are two ways to view the detailed property coverage information that was produced by the command line batch file. You can either inspect the contents of the plain text coverage files with a text editor or use the GUI (graphical user interface) that is available within VN-Property DX. This worked example will make use of the graphical user interface which can be invoked by entering the following text string.

```
C:\my-pc> vnavigator
```

This action will bring up a top-level flowchart, as shown in Figure F-1, to guide you through the various tools that are available within Verification Navigator's verification environment.

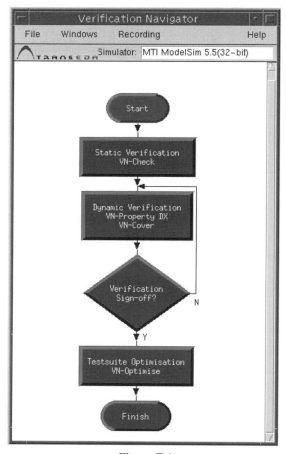

Figure F-1

The first button will invoke the Static Verification tool know as VN-Check. Further details on this particular tool can be found in Appendix B.

The second button will invoke the Dynamic Verification tool known as VN-Property DX. You should click this button to bring up another flowchart, as shown in Figure F-2 below. This flowchart is known as the Verification Flow and is designed to guide you through the various parts of the Dynamic Verification tool.

The third button will cause a window to be displayed that shows how many of the design units or modules have satisfied the user specified sign-off criteria.

The fourth button will invoke the Testsuite Optimisation tool know as VN-Optimise. Further information on this particular tool can be found in Chapter 12.

The Verification Flow flowchart, as shown in Figure F-2, is used to allow you to interact graphically with VN-Cover to create libraries, select the design files that you want to analyze and set up communication with your chosen simulator. As we have already generated the results file using the command line script (`doit.pc.bat`) you can skip this stage and move on to inspecting the dynamic coverage results.

Click the Results button - the sixth button the flowchart.

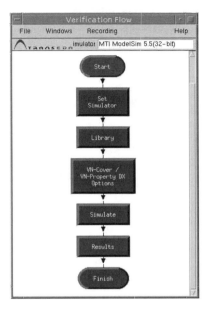

Figure F-2

This action will bring up the window as shown below.

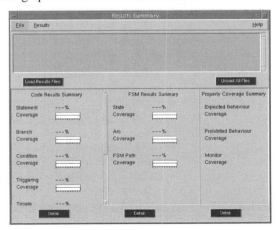

Figure F-3

Click the Load Results Files button to display the results files that are available.

Select the sub-directory labelled `vnavigator_files` and then select the results file `vnavigator_index` within that directory. This action will load the requested results file. A summary of the dynamic property coverage that has been achieved is displayed in the Results Summary window.

Figure F-4

Clicking the Detail button, at the base of the Results Summary window, will enable you to obtain detailed information about dynamic property coverage for the various sub-sequences in the design. The action of clicking the Detail button will cause the display screen to change and become populated with the set of six windows as shown in Figure F-5.

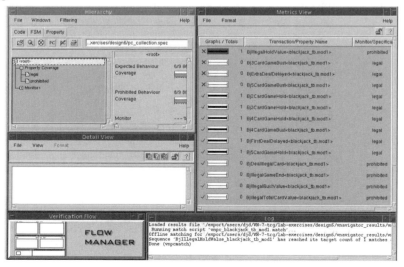

Figure F-5

The Flow Manager window is really an iconised version of the Verification Flow window and can be used as a way to return to the main flow if you need to repeat the instrumentation or simulation phases.

The right-hand section of the Hierarchy window, as shown in Figure F-6, shows a summary of the dynamic property coverage for the section of the design's hierarchy that is currently selected. At the moment the whole of the design's hierarchy (i.e. <root>) has been selected so what is indicated is a global summary for the property coverage for the whole design.

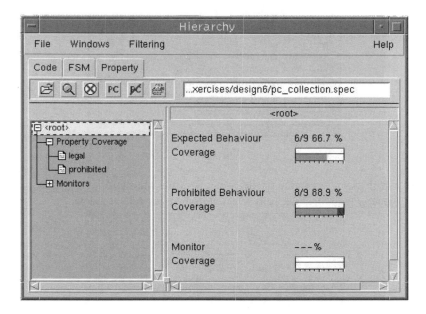

Figure F-6

Shown on the left-hand section of the Hierarchy window is a list of the libraries that VN-Cover visited and found to contain properties. In this particular case two libraries are listed which have the names: "legal" and "prohibited".

The right-hand section of the Hierarchy window gives a breakdown of the properties that have been categorized into the two classes of 'expected behaviour' and 'prohibited behaviour'.

A detailed list of which particular properties were satisfied or violated can be obtained by clicking each one of the libraries listed under the Property Coverage heading in the left-hand section of the Hierarchy window.

Figure F-7 shows an example of the contents of the Metrics View window after the library named *Legal* has been selected in the Hierarchy window. As can be seen in the figure below, three of the wanted or desired properties did not occur during the simulation and have been flagged as an error condition. All the other properties listed in the Metrics View window did occur at least once and therefore satisfied the property coverage criteria.

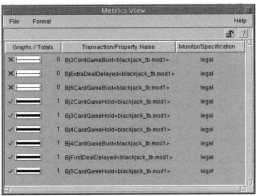

Figure F-7

Figure F-8 shows an example of the contents of the Metrics View window after the library named *Prohibited* has been selected in the Hierarchy window.

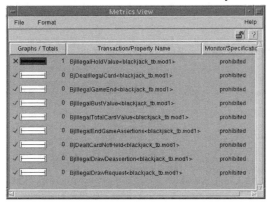

Figure F-8

As can be seen in the above figure, one of the prohibited or not wanted properties actually occurred during the simulation and was flagged as an error condition. All the other properties (shown in the Metrics View window) never occurred which satisfied this particular property coverage criteria.

Appendix G

Creating Properties

Worked Examples

This section presents some examples of how to create a set of files that can be used to check the dynamic property aspects of a simple finite state machine. It is assumed that you have already worked through Appendix F and have become familiar with using VN-Property DX to perform dynamic property checking.

GETTING ORGANIZED

The following files can be obtained as a single file in 'zip' format from TransEDA's web site at: www.transeda.com/vmm/

Create a directory (e.g. my-properties) on your system and then unpack the complete set of files that you obtained from TransEDA into that area.

fsm_test.v	// Verilog test bench
fsm.v	// Verilog code for the finite state machine
clk_gen.v	// Very simple 50-50 mark space ratio clock generator
pc_collection.spec	// Specifications collections file
doit.modelsim	// Script to perform functional coverage via the CLI

Please take a few moments to familiarise yourself with the contents of these files.

You should also have an additional set of files with the suffix .beh in this directory. These files contain the definitions for the various behaviors that are described in the remainder of this section.

BACKGROUND

A FSM is an electronic circuit that has a predictable or finite state that is based on a combination of the circuit's previous state and the circuit's current set of inputs. If you analyse the operation of today's electronic products you will discover that many of them are based on the concept of a finite state machine. A "hole in the wall" cash dispenser, a pedestrian controlled zebra crossing, a telephone answering machine, the fuel consumption distance/range recorder in a car are all examples of FSM based products.

OVERVIEW

The block diagram below shows part of the control system used to dispense hot drinks in a vending machine. It consists of a number of push buttons which are used to select the particular type of beverage (e.g. tea, coffee or hot chocolate) and additives (e.g. milk and/or sugar) required by the user. The state of the various push buttons is sensed by the control unit and used to operate a number of solenoids and pumps that heat the water and add the ingredients to the plastic cup. A set of indicator lights (also driven by the control unit) gives the user a visual indication of what is happening and when the drink is available for collection. A power-on reset signal is used to force the control unit into a known state when the vending machine is first switched-on.

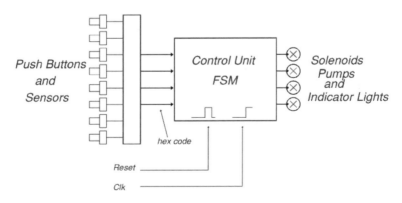

Figure G-1

The state diagram, shown below, defines the five possible states of the FSM and identifies the input conditions that cause the FSM to move from one state to another. It should be noted that the FSM will only make a change of state on the positive going edge of the clock pulse.

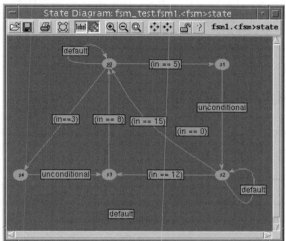

Figure G-2

Circular Tour

The first behavior we are going to look at is a test to check one of the circular tours around the FSM. We will assume that the FSM starts from state S0 and visits states S1, S2 and S3 (in that order) before returning to state S0. In this first example you can assume that the FSM is only allowed to loop on state S0. (i.e. it does not loop on any of the intervening states.) So the Perl quantifier list is: S0+ S1 S2 S3 S0+

Figure G-3 shows a listing of the file called `CircularTour.beh`. This example illustrates the use of the function ***Vector::integer*** which is used to determine the numerical value of the 'state' register.

You can check the operation of this behavior by simulating the design (`fsm.v` and `clk_gen.v`) with the test bench (`fsm_test.v`). You can either do this with VN-Property DX using the GUI or via the CLI using the script called `doit.modelsim`. In either case you will need to ensure that the appropriate behavior (i.e. `CircularTour.beh`) is called-up within the `pc_collection.spec` file. The results file should indicate that this particular behavior has been matched at least once.

Looping on S2

The next behavior that we are going to look at checks that the FSM starts from state S0 and visits state S1 before looping for a number of clock cycles on state S2. The Perl quantifier list for this behavior is: S0+ S1 S2{2,} Figure G-4 shows a listing of the file called LoopingOnS2.beh. This particular behavior uses a short subroutine called get_state() to return a text string that indicates the state of the 'state' register.

Counting the number of loops

The next behavior, as shown in Figure G-5, is a slightly modified version of the LoopingOnS2 behavior to count the actual number of times that S2 looped. It makes use of a User Data Block (UDB) and a user defined counter called S2Counter to record the actual number of times S2 looped.

This behavior also demonstrates how information that has been collected in the UDB can be printed out when a certain event has occurred.

Matching two lower level sequences

The next behavior, as shown in Figures G-6 to G-8, is designed to match two lower level behaviors and is implemented using three files. The first file called TopLevel.beh uses the match subsequence function (i.e. match_subseq) to check that the following two tours have been performed.

- S0+ S1 S2+ S0+

- S0+ S4 S3+ S0+

Using a Signals file

The final behavior, as shown in Figure G-10, that we will inspect makes use of a signals file to provide the user with a layer a of abstraction between the names of signals used within the properties and the names of signals used in the actual HDL implementation. It is effectively a mapping file. This means that if a signal name in the HDL implementation was changed then only the name in the signals file needs to be altered. This avoids having to go through every line in a behavior file looking for an out-of-date signal name.

Listing for a circular tour around the finite state machine.

```
package CircularTour;                    # Filename is "CircularTour.beh"
#define_clock fsm clk
use vars qw(@ISA);
@ISA = qw(Sequence);
sub begin
{
    my $self = shift;
    return
        {
            'steps' =>
                [
                    {
                        'test' => sub { Vector::integer(@fsm:state) == 0 },
                        'quantifier' => '+'
                    },

                    {
                        'test' => sub { Vector::integer(@fsm:state) == 1 },
                        'quantifier' => 1
                    },

                    {
                        'test' => sub { Vector::integer(@fsm:state) == 2 },
                        'quantifier' => 1
                    },

                    {
                        'test' => sub { Vector::integer(@fsm:state) == 3 },
                        'quantifier' => 1
                    },

                    {
                        'test' => sub { Vector::integer(@fsm:state) == 0 },
                        'quantifier' => '+'
                    },
                ]
        };
}
1;  # End of package file (must return 1)
```

Figure G-3

Listing to check looping on state S2 within the finite state machine.

```
package LoopingOnS2;                          # Filename is "LoopingOnS2.beh"
#define_clock fsm clk
use vars qw(@ISA);
@ISA = qw(Sequence);

sub begin
    {
        my $self = shift;
        return
            {
                'steps' =>
                    [
                        {
                            'info' => 'Waiting for state S0'
                            'test' => sub { ($self->get_state() eq 'S0') },
                            'quantifier' => '+'
                        },

                        {
                            'info' => 'Waiting for state S1'
                            'test' => sub { ($self->get_state() eq 'S1') },
                            'quantifier' => 1
                        },

                        {
                            'info' => 'Waiting for state S2'
                            'test' => sub { ($self->get_state() eq 'S2') },
                            'quantifier' => '2,'
                        },
                    ]
            };
    }

sub get_state
{
    my $self = shift;
    if   (Vector::integer(@fsm:state) == 0 {return 'S0'}
    elsif (Vector::integer(@fsm:state) == 1 {return 'S1'}
    elsif (Vector::integer(@fsm:state) == 2 {return 'S2'}
    elsif (Vector::integer(@fsm:state) == 3 {return 'S3'}
    elsif (Vector::integer(@fsm:state) == 4 {return 'S4'}
}
1;  # End of package file (must return 1)
```

Figure G-4

Listing to count how many times the finite state machine looped on S2.

```
package CountS2Loops                        # Filename is "CountS2Loops.beh"
#define_clock fsm clk
use vars qw(@ISA);
@ISA = qw(Sequence);

sub begin
{    my $self = shift;
     return
         {    'initial_data' =>  { 'S2Counter' => 0 },
              'steps' =>
                   [
                        { 'test' => sub { ($self->get_state() eq 'S2') }, 'quantifier' => 1},
                        { 'test' => sub { ($self->get_state() eq 'S2') }, 'quantifier' => '+',
                            'post_action' => sub
                                 { my ($user_data, $test_result) = @_;
                                      if ($test_result) { $user_data->{'S2Counter'} += 1; }
                                 }
                        },

                        { 'test' => sub { ($self->get_state() ne 'S2') },
                            'quantifier' => '+',
                            'post_action' => sub
                                 {    my $user_data = shift;
                                      my $counter_value = $user_data->{'S2Counter'};
                                      print "\n";
                                      print "The number of times S2 looped was $counter_value\n";
                                      print "\n";
                                      return 1;
                                 }
                        }
                   ]
         };
}

sub get_state
{
     my $self = shift;
     if    (Vector::integer(@fsm:state) == 0 {return 'S0'}
     elsif (Vector::integer(@fsm:state) == 1 {return 'S1'}
     elsif (Vector::integer(@fsm:state) == 2 {return 'S2'}
     elsif (Vector::integer(@fsm:state) == 3 {return 'S3'}
     elsif (Vector::integer(@fsm:state) == 4 {return 'S4'}
}
1;  # End of package file (must return 1)
```

Figure G-5

Listing to match two lower level sequences. Three files are needed to solve this particular situation. A top level sequence that calls the two lower level sequences.

The top level sequence is shown below.

```
package TopLevel                              # Filename is "TopLevel.beh"
#define_clock fsm clk
use vars qw(@ISA);
@ISA = qw(Sequence);

# Load the lower-level sub-sequence packages
use Tour0120;
use Tour0430;

sub begin
{
    my $self = shift;

    # Instantiate the sub-sequences
    $self->{'0120'} = Tour0120->new();
    $self->{'0430'} = Tour0430->new();
    return

    # Sequence data structure
        {
            'steps' =>
                [
                    {
                        'test' =>
                            sub {
                                    $self->match_subseq
                                    (
                                        $self->{'0120'}, $self->{'0430'}
                                    )
                                },
                            'quantifier' => '+'
                    }
                ]
        };
}
1;  # End of TopLevel package file (must return 1)
```

Figure G-6

Listing of the lower level sequence to check the circular tour S0+ S1 S2+ S0+

```
package Tour0120                          # Filename is "Tour0120.beh"
#define_clock fsm clk
use vars qw(@ISA);
@ISA = qw(Sequence);

sub begin
{
    my $self = shift;
    return
        {
            'steps' =>
                [
                    {
                        'test' => sub { ($self->get_state() eq 'S0') }, 'quantifier' => '+'
                    },

                    {
                        'test' => sub { ($self->get_state() eq 'S1') }, 'quantifier' => 1
                    },

                    {
                        'test' => sub { ($self->get_state() eq 'S2') }, 'quantifier' => '+'
                    },

                    {
                        'test' => sub { ($self->get_state() eq 'S0') }, 'quantifier' => '+'
                    },
                ]
        };
}

sub get_state
{
    my $self = shift;
    if    (Vector::integer(@fsm:state) == 0 {return 'S0'}
    elsif (Vector::integer(@fsm:state) == 1 {return 'S1'}
    elsif (Vector::integer(@fsm:state) == 2 {return 'S2'}
    elsif (Vector::integer(@fsm:state) == 3 {return 'S3'}
    elsif (Vector::integer(@fsm:state) == 4 {return 'S4'}
}

1;  # End of package file (must return 1)
```

Listing G-7

Listing of the lower level sequence to check the circular tour S0+ S4 S3+ S0+

```
package Tour0430                              # Filename is "Tour0430.beh"
#define_clock fsm clk
use vars qw(@ISA);
@ISA = qw(Sequence);

sub begin
{
    my $self = shift;
    return
        {
            'steps' =>
                [
                    {
                        'test' => sub { ($self->get_state() eq 'S0') }, 'quantifier' => '+'
                    },

                    {
                        'test' => sub { ($self->get_state() eq 'S4') }, 'quantifier' => 1
                    },

                    {
                        'test' => sub { ($self->get_state() eq 'S3') }, 'quantifier' => '+'
                    },

                    {
                        'test' => sub { ($self->get_state() eq 'S0') }, 'quantifier' => '+'
                    },
                ]
        };
}

sub get_state
{
    my $self = shift;
    if    (Vector::integer(@fsm:state) == 0  {return 'S0'}
    elsif (Vector::integer(@fsm:state) == 1  {return 'S1'}
    elsif (Vector::integer(@fsm:state) == 2  {return 'S2'}
    elsif (Vector::integer(@fsm:state) == 3  {return 'S3'}
    elsif (Vector::integer(@fsm:state) == 4  {return 'S4'}
}

1;  # End of package file (must return 1)
```

Figure G-8

Listing to check the circular tour S0+ S1 S2 S3 S0+

This sequence uses a signals file to map signal names to the HDL implementation.

```
package MySignalsTour                    # Filename is "MySignalsTour.beh"
use vars qw(@ISA);
@ISA = qw(Sequence);

use FSMsignals;

sub begin
{
    my $self = shift;
    return
        {
            'steps' =>
                [
                    { 'test' => sub { FSMsignals::Idle()   == 1 }, 'quantifier' => '+' },

                    { 'test' => sub { FSMsignals::Coffee() == 1 }, 'quantifier' => 1 },

                    { 'test' => sub { FSMsignals::Milk()   == 1 }, 'quantifier' => 1 },

                    { 'test' => sub { FSMsignals::Sugar()  == 1 }, 'quantifier' => 1 },

                    { 'test' => sub { FSMsignals::Idle()   == 1 }, 'quantifier' => '+' },
                ]
        };
}
1;  # End of package file (must return 1)
```

Figure G-9

Layout of the signals file

```
package FSMsignals                       # Filename is "FSMsignals.beh"

#define_clock fsm clk

# Basic signals...
sub Idle        { (Vector::integer(@fsm:state) == 0) }
sub Coffee      { (Vector::integer(@fsm:state) == 1) }
sub Milk        { (Vector::integer(@fsm:state) == 2) }
sub Sugar       { (Vector::integer(@fsm:state) == 3) }
sub Tea         { (Vector::integer(@fsm:state) == 4) }

1; # End of FSMsignals package
```

Figure G-10

This page is intentionally left blank.

Glossary

A GLOSSARY OF EDA AND CAE TERMS

Accellera
The Accellera Formal Verification Technical Committee has been created to develop and promote a property specification language compatible with Verilog (IEEE-1364) and VHDL (IEEE-1076). Visit: *www.accellera.org* for further information.

ADA
A programming language.

ASCII
American Standard Code for Information Interchange, the encoding scheme for text files, each character is represented by a 1 byte number.

ASIC
Application Specific Integrated Circuit, a silicon chip custom designed for a specific purpose.

Behavior
A specification of signal values over time. For example, "the signal *req* is true for three cycles; on the fourth cycle the signal *req* is still true and the signal *ack* is false."

Behavior coverage
The percentage of expected behaviors detected by the checker in the dynamic results. This applies to both data coverage and temporal behavior. Behavior coverage is a user-defined metric that typically reflects the contents of the verification plan. The verification engineer defines a set of behaviors that the system must be tested for. For example, if the system can read and write data, to several memory blocks

Branch coverage
Coverage measurement also known as block coverage, it checks each branch in a branching construct such as an 'if' or 'case' statement has been tested.

BFMs
Bus functional models, a piece of software designed to mimic the behavior of a hardware interface device.

Coverage analysis   A technique for measuring how much of the source code of a computer program or hardware description has been executed by a test run or simulation.

Control file   A file which is the cross reference between the coverage analysis results file (history file) and the original HDL source code (Verification Navigator specific).

Core   Also called IP Cores these are hardware descriptions of a piece of reusable hardware, such as a Pentium processor model. These can be incorporated into a larger design.

Design rule checker A software tool that performs static checks on HDL.

DFT   Design For Test
                    An approach that is used during the design phase of an IC that concentrates on providing a means of testing an integrated circuit after it has been manufactured.

DUT   Design (or Device) Under Test, this is the circuit description which is being tested by simulation.

Dynamic check   A technique of checking a set of properties from a set of simulation results. Note: The fact that the property holds for the set of simulation results is not a proof that the property is true for the system.

Dynamic property   A technique that checks that a design does or does not conform to
checking   a specified property for a set of stimuli.

Dynamic   Exercising a model or models of a design, or a hardware
verification   implementation of the design with a set of stimuli.

Expected behavior   A behaviour that should occur in the design. This behavior is reported as "covered" if the dynamic results exhibit it.
                    See also prohibited behavior.

Fault Simulation   This is a simulation technique used to verify the effectiveness of test patterns which will be used to evaluate the manufactured device. Usually the fault model used assumes that each node in the circuit is either shorted to power (stuck-at-1) or ground (stuck-at-0). The fault simulator tests that simulation results are different for a fault free circuit and a circuit with a fault.

FEC	Focused Expression Coverage, a coverage measurement for Boolean expressions which only requires $N + 1$ test patterns, where N is the number of inputs to the expression, instead of the 2^N maximum number of input combinations.
Formal verification	Use of various types of logic and mathematical methods to verify the correctness of IC logic or system interactions. Equivalence checking is the most common formal verification method, which is used to compare the design that is being created against a design that is already proven accurate.
FSM	Finite State Machine An electronic circuit that has a predictable or finite state that is based on a combination of the circuit's previous state and the circuit's current set of inputs.
FSM arc coverage	A technique for checking that every arc or transition between states within a FSM has been traversed.
FSM coverage	A technique for measuring how much of a FSM has been covered in respect of state-coverage, arc-coverage and path-coverage.
FSM cycle	A cycle is a directed set of states that returns to its starting state without passing through any state more than one.
FSM link	A directed set of states that does not repeat. An example would be an initialization sequence.
FSM path coverage	Visited state and arc coverage do not necessarily measure the extent to which the functionality of a FSM has been verified. The more powerful path coverage metric measures that all the paths or routes through a sequence of visited states or arcs in the FSM have actually been taken.
FSM state coverage	A technique for checking that every state of a FSM has been visited. Often referred to as "visited state coverage."
FSM supercycle	A longer cycle (than an FSM cycle) that identifies the high level functionality and provides a concise summary of the overall structure of the FSM.
Gate level	The point in the design process where the circuit is completely described as an interconnection of logic gates, such as NAND, NOR and D-type registers.
Graphical editors	A software tool that enables the architecture and definition of a design to be captured graphically.

HDL   Hardware Description Language, a programming language like
                       way of describing hardware. The two most common HDL's are
                       Verilog and VHDL.

Instrument   To instrument an HDL circuit description is the process of adding
                       extra HDL code to determine what has been executed during the
                       simulation.

IP   Intellectual Property or IP Cores these are hardware descriptions
                       of a piece of reusable hardware, such as a Pentium processor
                       model. These can be incorporated into a larger design.

JTAG   Joint Test Access Group
                       A consortium of individuals from North American companies
                       whose objective is to tackle the challenges of testing high density
                       IC devices.

Linters   A software tool that performs a predefined set of fixed checks on
                       a coding language such as Verilog, VHDL, C or C++.

Logic synthesis   The process of converting a RTL (Register Transfer Level)
                       hardware description to gate level, this is usually automated by
                       software tools.

Model checking   A   formal   verification   technique   that   compares   the
                       implementation of a design to a set of user-specified properties.
                       Determines whether a set of properties hold true for the given
                       implementation of a design. If the property is false, a counter-
                       example is produced. Also referred to as property checking.

Netlist   A circuit description which consists of a list of interconnected
                       sub-blocks, they can be written in Verilog, VHDL or a variety of
                       standard and proprietary netlist languages.

OpenMORE   Open Measure Of Reuse Excellence. A design scoring system
                       devised by Mentor and Synopsys.
                       Visit *www.openmore.com* for full details.

Pascal   A programming language.

Path coverage   A coverage measurement which checks that all the paths through
                       consecutive branching constructs in procedural blocks are tested.

Perl   A programming language.

Post-simulation   A technique that allows the elimination of coverage analysis
results filtering   errors that are associated with unreachable or unexecutable HDL

Probe	A software 'monitor' point which is included in an HDL description for the purpose of collecting coverage analysis information.
Prohibited behavior	A behavior that should not occur in the design. A violation of prohibited behavior is reported if the dynamic results exhibit the behaviour.
Property	A statement that a given behavior is "expected" or "prohibited."
Property coverage	Property checking supported by behavior coverage. This is the association between a property and the scenarios in which the property should be checked. Scenarios are described by means of expected behaviors.
Property checking	A formal verification technique that verifies that a design does or does not conform to a specified property under all possible sets of legal input conditions. Like HDL rule checking, the design is checked for conformance with one or more properties producing errors called violations where the design does not conform to the property.
RMM	Reuse Methodology Manual A set of guidelines that define good coding styles for HDL design. See Appendix A for more details.
RTL	Register Transfer Level, the point where the design is written as a register transfer description. A register transfer description is a type of a behavioral description which is closely related to the hardware implementation. The description is written in terms of register banks and combinational logic.
Rule-based checkers	A software tool that performs static checks on HDL by applying a set of rules (defined by one or more rule-databases) that have been selected and customised by the user.
State diagram	Graphical method of showing the pictorial representation of a structure and interaction within a finite state machine.
SoC	System on a Chip. The term used to describe the large scale integration of a complete system onto a single piece of silicon.
Statement coverage	Also known as line coverage, this is a coverage analysis metric which checks the number of executable statement that have actually been executed in the HDL description being tested.

Synthesis	See logic synthesis.
Tabular trace	A method of recording the results from a simulation run in a compact tabular or column orientated format. Information is only recorded when a change occurs on a traced signal. Often referred to as a trace file or tab file.
TAP controller	Test Access Port controller A design that is often used as a benchmark within the EDA industry for checking the performance of FSM coverage analysis tools. A TAP controller is a state machine (with 16 possible states) that is used to control operations associated with the boundary scan cells (that appear on the periphery) of an integrated circuit.
Test bench	A set of stimuli (plus response checking) that is used to check the correct operation of a circuit description.
Test suite analysis	A technique for sorting the test benches, used in the regression suite, in the most productive order so that the test bench that gives the maximum amount of coverage in the minimum amount of simulation time is ranked the highest in the list. The process is repeated on an iterative basis until all the test benches have been analyzed. Non-productive test benches are not included in the final list.
Test suite optimization	See test suite analysis.
Text editors	A software tool that enables text files to be created and modified.
Toggle coverage	A coverage measurement which checks that each bit of a signal has switched between logic-0 and logic-1 (or vice versa) and back again.
Verilog	A hardware description language.
VHDL	VHSIC Hardware Description Language.
VHSIC	Very High Speed Integrated Circuit.

Index

AN INDEX OF TOPICS IN THIS BOOK

Design rule checker, 132
Design rule checkers, 10
Design rules
    attributes, 14
    coding, 10
    databases of, 10
    documentation, 10
    examples, 14
    naming, 10
    style, 10
Design specification, 24
Design steps, 2
Device Under Test, 102, 115
Directed expression coverage, 46
Documentation rules, 10
Duplicate tests, 120
DUT, 102, 115
Dynamic property checking, 95, 99

E
ECO
    engineering change orders, 129
Editors
    graphical, 9
    text, 8
Exclude code, 59, 74
Expected behavior, 182
Exponential growth in testing time, 48
Expression Coverage, 44

F
Fault simulation, 26, 70
FEC, 46
Filtered code
    at different levels in a hierarchy, 63
    identifying, 62
    information about, 62
Focused Expression Coverage, 46, 74
FSM, 79
    coverage, 79
    cycle, 82
    link, 82
    path coverage, 80

M

N

O

P

V

Variable trace coverage, 54
Verification flow, 98
Verification Navigator, 135
    evaluation copy, 132
Visual checking, 96
VN-Check design rule checker, 132, 135
    evaluation copy, 132
VN-Property DX, 102, 132

W

Web sites, 131
White box testing, 40
Wildcards, 81